I0531223

A CINEPHILE UNDER THE INFLUENCE

A CINEPHILE UNDER THE INFLUENCE

David Sterritt

Conversations with Mikita Brottman

Sticking Place Books
New York

© David Sterritt and Mikita Brottman 2025
© Sticking Place Books 2025

Cover image © Fred Camper

www.stickingplacebooks.com

All rights reserved.

No part of this book may be reproduced, stored in or introduced into a
retrieval system, or transmitted, in any form or by any means (electronic,
mechanical, photocopying, recording or otherwise) without the written
permission of the publishers, except in the case of brief quotations embodied
in critical articles or reviews.

ISBN 979-8-89976-029-7

To Mikita, and Jeremy and Craig,
and Tanya and Kim
(and Brutus, of course)

CONTENTS

REVIEWER, PROFESSOR, ET CETERA
BY WHEELER WINSTON DIXON

David Sterritt is one of my favorite critical voices on the history and practice of cinema, primarily because he uses direct and accessible language in his writing in addition to having such excellent taste. I've known him for a long time, and he's one of the greats. I'm also struck by how often David and I agree on the merits—or lack thereof—of a given film, whether it's underrated, as is the case with Floyd Mutrux's unjustly obscure musical biopic *American Hot Wax* (1978), or overrated: Howard Hawks's *Red Line 7000* (1965), Alfred Hitchcock's *Torn Curtain* (1966), Stanley Kubrick's *A Clockwork Orange* (1971), among others. Even when I disagree with David on a film, as in the case of Martin Scorsese's *The Last Temptation of Christ* [1988] (I love it, he doesn't), I never feel that he is forcing his own view at the expense of other possible interpretations. He cuts to the heart of what any given film is trying to accomplish and what knowledge it wants to impart to the viewer. In this volume, prompted by Mikita Brottman's incisive questions, David offers the real rundown on his life as a major film critic during cinema's most exciting era.

David and I were both privileged to work in what may possibly be the last truly Golden Age of the cinema, the period from its inception to the early 2000s. Before the advent of digital technology, film was an entirely analog experience: shot on film, printed in huge batches of prints (35mm for theatrical presentation, 16mm for colleges and film societies), advertised with one-sheet posters and lobby cards, and available only when one went to a theater to see that specific work. The beauty of silver nitrate film prints, the cinematic medium used for all films before the introduction of safety film in 1950, is a shimmering sheen of visual splendor that pops off the screen. No digital process will ever create such an experience for the audience. When I worked as a film critic in the last days of *Life* magazine and during the birth of Andy Warhol's *Interview* in the late 1960s, films were shown only in screening rooms, in the original 35mm format, with IATSE union projectionists who ensured that the image was sharp, bright, and flawlessly presented on the screen. It's really the only way to truly see a film. Now, of course, "screeners" and video links are much more of a factor, especially for foreign and independent films, but no matter the medium, David sees the film for what it truly is, what it truly *intends*, and what it values.

As film critic for *The Christian Science Monitor* from 1968 until his retirement in 2005, David reviewed thousands of films and was known for championing avant-garde cinema, theater, and music. He was the film critic for NPR's *All Things Considered* (1978–1980), the Boston theater critic for *Variety* (1969–1973), and the video critic for *Islands* magazine (2000–2003). He served as a film professor in Columbia University's School of the Arts and is now professor emeritus of theater and film at Long Island University and an adjunct professor at the Maryland Institute College of Art. He chaired the National Society of Film Critics from 2005 to 2015, served two terms as chair of the New York Film Critics Circle, and was on the selection committee for the New York Film Festival (1988–1992). When Gwendolyn Audrey Foster and I resigned our positions as editors in chief of *Quarterly Review of Film and Video* after a fifteen-year stint (1999–2014), we had no question about whom we wanted to succeed us, and David took over the editorship of the journal with his usual style and elan from 2014 to 2023.

David has also written and edited numerous influential books on film and culture, including *The Films of Alfred Hitchcock* (1993), *The Films of Jean-Luc Godard: Seeing the Invisible* (1999), *Jean-Luc Godard: Interviews* (editor, 1998), *Mad to Be Saved: The Beats, the '50s, and Film* (1998), *The Cinema of Clint Eastwood: Chronicles of America* (2014), and *Simply Hitchcock* (2017). He has also contributed numerous essays to Criterion's state-of-the-art DVD collection, with pieces on such films as Terry Gilliam's *Time Bandits* (1981), Lars von Trier's *Breaking the Waves* (1996), and John Frankenheimer's *Seconds* (1966). And more, all while keeping his eye on the horizon to see what's coming next.

With all of this, David has undoubtedly created a significant body of work in the field of film criticism, and his writing is some of the clearest, most deeply personal and thoughtful work that one can find. It's deeply meditational. When David views a film, he takes it apart on numerous levels simultaneously: editing, lighting, music, shot design, acting, direction, and anything else that seems central to an understanding of the film in question. Although he's basically an auteurist—someone who believes that the director is the primary motivating force behind a film—David nevertheless knows the limits and pitfalls of this critical position. Just because a director's string of films has a distinct visual and aesthetic style, that doesn't mean *every* film by that director lives up to the previous work.

What David always seeks is the *intelligence* behind a film, the motivating force that brought about that film's existence. He does away with arbitrary and restrictive categories like "A" and "B" films, big budget movies and small art house films, or "foreign" as opposed to Hollywood films. There are infinite levels to examine in any film—cultural, political, social, and sexual, to name a few—and there is also the technical virtuosity, or lack thereof, with which the film is made. No matter his ultimate opinion, David comes down firmly in his judgments. I do the same thing: I hold that certain values in a film deserve to be celebrated and examined, and generally I trust my judgment in these matters to be correct. David is perfectly happy if a reader disagrees with his opinions. He wants to be the person who introduces you to a given film and shares his thoughts on it; your opinion may differ, which is fine.

Watching David watch a film is a real experience. He insists that the atmosphere should be quiet and respectful. As he points out, "movies demand the respect of quiet, undisturbed surroundings, at least for critics who'll be opining and passing judgment on them." He keeps his comments during screenings to a minimum, quietly embracing the film on the screen. His opinions after screenings are swift and insightful, and he writes honestly and from the heart. If David loves a film, you'll know it; if he hates it, you'll know that too. Wherever he falls along the continuum, he shares his reactions. And to my mind, he's also a very kind critic, in the best possible way, despite his stated belief to the contrary. As he puts it, "I don't particularly think of myself as a generous or forgiving critic, but I suppose it's relatively rare to find a movie that's totally awful in every way, so I'll probably try to mention whatever glimmer of light manages to make its way into a generally rotten picture."

Yet David doesn't hold anything back when he really feels disappointed in a film, even if he knows the filmmaker personally. As he notes in this interview, "a television critic I knew told me that if stating a negative opinion means upsetting a friend, he chooses the friend over the opinion. Not me! But I admit I may try to soften the blow a bit by using measured language." No matter what one might think of David's opinion, he's forthright about it. As a critic, it's his job to discuss the film and then give his general assessment. It comes with the territory. But he never resorts to a hatchet job. He tries to find the best in any film he reviews. In many ways, David is unique as a film critic in combining the requirements of a daily reviewer (in his capacity as critic for *The Christian Science Monitor*, for example) with the skill and knowledge of a long-form critic, one who takes a deep dive into the material. His reviews never seem hammered out; he genuinely engages with the films he covers, for better or worse.

Although he says he doesn't have an overall philosophy of criticism, feeling that "having a philosophy of criticism seems a little grand, [although] I have ideas that add up to an informal philosophy," David clearly feels a responsibility to be true to the spirit of a film—good, bad, or indifferent—above any other considerations. As he puts it, "whatever the venue is, I think the critic's opinion of a film—did I like it, did I hate it, did it make me laugh or cry or get hungry or want to get the hell out—is far less important than the information I convey *about* the film […] Even if I strongly signal that I like or dislike the film, readers should be given enough information to form their own provisional opinions, which may go in the opposite direction: Sterritt loved it but I can tell from his review that I'd hate it, or Sterritt hated it but his review makes me think I'd love it. My bottom-line yea or nay matters, but it's not what matters most in the review."

David is also justly suspicious of film criticism that seems more in love with abstruse systems than with actual interpretation. As he puts it, "I've written quite a bit in that area, partly because of personal interest and partly because it's been a trend in academic film criticism and analysis. I must say this trend has been somewhat amusing to me. As self-aware academics have occasionally recognized, some cinema scholars have an inferiority complex—they're not part of a centuries-old enterprise like literary criticism or music criticism, and they deal with movies, which are notoriously enmeshed in popular culture rather than high culture. Hence the infatuation cinema scholars fell into for a while with semiotics and psychoanalysis, which allow them to conduct abstruse analyses with the aid of special-ized vocabularies and recondite conceptual frameworks." This, as David suggests, results in less-than-enlightening discourse. When a critical apparatus is allowed to over-whelm a film, the work being considered can get lost in the discussion, and David will have none of that.

Above all, David believes in encouraging "more *adven-turous* moviegoing. Even casual moviegoers have much to gain by looking beyond Hollywood hits and giving a shot to challenging art films, productions from the silent era, films from far-flung countries, and avant-garde works that require active thinking by the viewer. Cinema is a vast and varied artform. Let a zillion flowers bloom!" That's precisely what he does in his work. Usually, he readily comes down with his opinions on a film, but occasionally he goes through a complete reversal, as was the case with Kubrick's *The Shining* (1980). On his first viewing, David found *The Shining* "somewhat chilly… rather distant and certainly not as horrifying as a first-rate horror movie should be. I was talking with Brian De Palma not long after the screening, and I gave him the opinion I just gave you, and he was very interested because he hadn't seen the picture yet. Later it turned out that Stephen King [quite famously] had a similar view, as he told me when I interviewed him."

But on the second screening of *The Shining*, in what he describes as less-than-ideal circumstances, David notes that "from the first moments I was blown away by it. The traveling shots at the beginning transfixed me, and I stayed transfixed right to the end. How could I have been so thick-headed the first time I saw it? My theory is that I'd recently read King's novel for the first time, and it was very present in my mind, interfering in some strange way with my perceptions of the film as it unfolded. But that's no excuse. I was thickheaded, period. In dramatic, cinematic, and narrative terms *The Shining* is a magisterial achievement, as many subsequent viewings have amply confirmed." So David's not afraid to change his mind or to admit it publicly—the sign of a truly great critic. As Dr. Samuel Johnson so aptly put it, "When the facts change, I change my opinion. How about you, Sir?" Clearly, although some films greatly impress David on first impact, others require a longer period of introspection, and he is happy to admit it. As always, the *film*, not personal opinion, is the center of discussion.

David has his favorite filmmakers: Jean-Luc Godard, for example, with his white-hot series of films in the 1960s, starting with *À Bout de souffle* (known as *Breathless* in the UK and US, 1960) and continuing through *Vivre sa vie* (*My Life to Live*, 1962), the lavishly beautiful *Le Mépris* (*Contempt*, 1963)—surely one of the greatest films about the actual filmmaking process, starring Fritz Lang as the director of a morally compromised version of *The Odyssey* for an egomaniacal producer played with bombastic relish by Jack Palance—and his eerily prescient dystopian vision of a future society ruled by computers (imagine that!) in *Alphaville* (1965), with Eddie Constantine as secret agent Lemmy Caution, whose mission is to destroy the machine. But David has little patience for Godard's overtly political work with the Dziga Vertov group, which often seems wilfully didactic and engaged in obfuscation. So again, auteurism is at work here, but when that initial vision is modified and/or abandoned, David's consideration of a director's work begins anew, jettisoning older models that no longer seem to apply.

David loves Hitchcock—certainly more than I do. Although only a philistine would deny the power of such films as *Shadow of a Doubt* (1943) or the most obvious example, *Psycho* (1960), David can also find something to like in Hitchcock's last—and to my mind, least interesting—film, *Family Plot* (1976), which seems more than a bit of a stretch. Yet every time one might feel that David has gone off on a bit of a tangent, one is cognizant of the fact that his foundation remains rock solid. Truffaut, Bergman, Fellini, and other key international directors; the American masters such as John Ford, Charles Chaplin, and Josef von Sternberg; and numerous other luminaries from cinema's past are key figures for him. As he puts it, "movies—good movies, and sometimes not-so-good ones—[are] products of both individual artistry and what the great André Bazin called the genius of the system." Bazin's pioneering magazine *Cahiers du cinéma* fostered the idea of "la politique des auteurs," and to properly apply that set of values, one must have a comprehensive knowledge of the field. In this respect, David has few if any peers; his knowledge of the history and practice of film is encyclopedic.

David is also deeply conscious that every era of film history has a different flavor: the busy industrialism of the 1920s on a worldwide basis, including Soviet cinema; the pre-Code 1930s, when the studio system solidified in the midst of the Depression; the noir 1940s, when such talents as Jacques Tourneur and Howard Hawks created some of the most memorable films in this dystopian genre; the paranoid and escapist 1950s; the worldwide explosion of new talents and new ways of thinking about narrative construction in the 1960s, as evidenced in films as disparate as Bergman's *Persona* (1966) and John Boorman's *Point Blank* (1967); the somewhat disillusioned and hypercapitalist 1980s; and into the twenty-first century, when film itself was abandoned for all intents and purposes in favor of digital spectacle, captured on hard drives rather than celluloid. Each era requires a different set of tools to unpack a given film; it's a pleasure to watch David dive in and come out with fresh and unique perspectives.

Cinema used to be destination viewing; now it's everywhere, and the smaller, more thoughtful films are lost in the marketplace, getting streaming-only releases (if that) and sometimes not finding distributors at all. The multiplexes are dominated by blockbuster spectacle, franchise films, comic-book movies, and horror films, which are cheap to make, don't rely on star power, and can captivate viewers with ever-increasing doses of violence. At the same time, we're no longer a *reading* culture, and reviews have devolved into the "thumbs up, thumbs down" ratings on Rotten Tomatoes and other review sites that aggregate the critical consensus of a given film into a brief numerical rating. True discussions of films in the media are increasingly rare. Sadly, many of the film-criticism journals that proliferated in the 1950s through the early 2000s are now gone, replaced by instant-read one-line reviews that don't delve into the content of a film. As a result, David's work is even more valuable to the present-day reader. In addition to this volume of his thoughts on the passing cinematic parade, it would be nice to see all of David's writing collected in one volume—properly indexed, of course. It would probably top out at more than 1,000 pages. What a resource that would be for scholars in the future!

So here is David's memoir, in effect; the result of spending an entire life in the service of film. Only with this kind of total immersion can one truly begin to understand the cinema, where it has been, and where it's going now in the digital era. The theaters in which both David and I spent much of our earlier lives are now long gone. In the New Yorker, the Thalia, and many other Manhattan venues, triple bills were not unusual, and patrons would line up around the block to see the latest international or Hollywood film, or perhaps a revival of a classic from the past. There's really nothing like seeing a film with an engaged and enthusiastic audience. But what once was a public art, routinely seen by millions of dedicated viewers in theaters, has now been transformed into something both special and precious, often seen on home flatscreen televisions with just a few friends. It's an entirely different viewing experience, and intelligent discussion of films is often lacking. That's another reason why David's work is so important, and why it urgently requires our attention.

David's writing chronicles an era in film history that will not come again. In this book we can see how he approaches a film, how he analyzes it, how he weighs the various factors that go into its production—in short, we get a real look at the working life of a film critic. It is one person's view of the twentieth-century's most lively and accessible art form; someone who knows what he's talking about and has translated his insights into informed criticism that documents the cinema in all its high and low points. It is an essential and invaluable volume offering the "inside scoop" on the life and work of one of the cinema's most influential and important critics. It's also a blast to read. So turn the page and see what an astonishing career David Sterritt has had, and how he continues his work in the present day. You're in for an amazing and enlightening experience. *Vive le cinéma!*

Wheeler Winston Dixon is a writer and filmmaker.

INTRODUCTION
BY MIKITA BROTTMAN

I should begin by stating that I'm David's partner, and some readers might consider me too partial to be the interviewer for this book. But as a film scholar and cultural critic myself, I'd suggest I'm more than qualified as a collaborator. Who else could have a better knowledge of David's life and work than someone who has witnessed a great deal of it—twenty-five years' worth—at first hand? Perhaps like all criticism, moreover, his work is grounded in autobiography, and I am uniquely positioned to discern where the life merges with the work.

David compares his career to "a big overstuffed chair that you've been sitting in for years and years, so its contours have shaped to your body and it fits you just right, although it wouldn't fit anybody else." What I particularly like about this metaphor is that it suggests not only longevity, but also comfort and pleasure, as well as the fact that David's career has been driven more by serendipity than by long-term plans. In my questions, I try to bring this out. Apart from everything else, I hope the readers of this book gets a sense of how much David has enjoyed his unique career, and how much gratification it has brought to him, as well as to his readers, his interview subjects, his audiences, his students, and his colleagues. To spend every day in the company of someone whose life's work has brought him so much pleasure is inspirational to me.

This book presents a compelling and detailed account of David's wide-ranging career, encompassing over fifty years of criticism, reviews, interviews, academic articles, essays, and lectures on all aspects of cinema, highbrow and lowbrow, mainstream and avant-garde. Additionally—and many readers of his film writing may be unaware of this fact—David has always been a well-regarded critic of other arts, too: music, dance, theater, the visual arts, and even the Moscow circus! As he points out, "I'd rather give my attention to a first-rate theater piece or a first-rate piece of music than to a third- or fourth-rate movie."

My first question deals with whether David has a philosophy of film criticism. We return to that at the end, but in essence, what drives and energizes the book is finding the answer to this question. In the process we consider David's career in a chronological fashion, beginning with his childhood and how he first became interested in the cinematic arts. As he explains, his attention was first aroused by television (an attention that never went away—in his later life, he wrote a book on the 1950s sitcom *The Honeymooners*, a longtime favorite). In terms of schooling, we talk about David's formal education (although in some ways he is an autodidact as well as a polymath), including his formative years at Boston University. Later, in his forties, he acquired a PhD in cinema studies at NYU, although as he notes, much of his experience there "did not pay particularly high dividends."

David is best known for his nearly forty years as film critic for *The Christian Science Monitor*, from 1968 until his retirement in 2005, which he describes succinctly as a "good berth." The *Monitor*, of course, has a high reputation, particularly (and partly thanks to David) for its reliable and influential arts reviews. At least until the 2000s, as David recounts, this provided fulfilling and satisfying work with (mostly) accommodating colleagues who allowed him (frequently) a healthy amount of freedom. As with any publication, there were sometimes obsessive and self-important editors as well as certain fastidious folks who ensured his work did not contravene Christian Science's frustrating taboos, such as occasional bans on words like "dead" and "die" and avoidance of "potentially offensive content." (As David notes, it was ironic that, while he was writing for the *Monitor*, one of his closest colleagues was the critic for *Playboy* magazine.)

At the *Monitor* David began in an entry-level nonwriting job in the Boston newsroom, feeling privileged, as he notes, to have known and worked in the "old hot-type setup." His career as a critic has encompassed a wide range of technical developments, from projected movies to home video and DVDs and thence to digital cinema, streaming, and films made for online formats. Some of the "old guard" critics might hesitate to call this "progress," but David, always open to new ideas, is no "film-on-film purist," generously acknowledging that all formats have their pros and cons. (And on the subject of technical developments, David has a secret and endearing affection for "processes and gimmicks" like 3D, Cinerama, Sensurround, and even Odorama).

The 1970s, when David began establishing himself at the *Monitor*, was, as he notes, "a great time to be a journalist." This period encompassed his move to New York, his discovery and subsequent lifelong fascination with minimalism as expressed in the work of theater companies like The Wooster Group, stage directors such as Robert Wilson, musicians such as Philip Glass and Steve Reich, and others. The 1970s were also the heady days of junkets—perks like international travel, celebrity-studded dinners and parties, and even (during a visit to the set of the movie *The Deep* in Bermuda) a private scuba-diving trip. As David acknowledges, this practice has now been largely and appropriately discontinued, but clearly, it was fun while it lasted.

Film festivals are a more serious matter. In Cannes, Telluride, Palm Springs, Moscow, Sarasota, and elsewhere (sometimes as part of FIPRESCI, the International Federation of Film Critics), David has discovered (often bringing to world attention) unknown gems from foreign directors. I've accompanied David to a few of these festivals, and I can assure you, they are not all basking in the sun and drinking cocktails (at least, not for David). For critics on the festival jury, they can be grinding work, featuring multiple screenings a day and jury meetings late into the evening.

Even outside film festivals, David has always been an ardent supporter of films from countries not well known for their national cinemas (at least, not in the U.S.), including under-recognized productions from Czechoslovakia, Iran, Japan, Italy, Brazil, Chile, Mexico, and elsewhere. On many occasions, his insightful writing about such movies has helped cement an actor's or director's reputation in the U.S. On native soil too, while David has plenty to say about box-office hits (and box-office failures, which, as he points out, can be artistic successes), he has always been drawn to smaller, independently made films screened in arthouse theaters.

Small names are counterbalanced by big ones. Those curious about celebrities will find plenty of inside scoops here. David has interviewed some of the greatest names in cinema. Just a few: Alfred Hitchcock, George Cukor, David Niven, Gene Kelly, Sophia Loren, Kirk Douglas, Gregory Peck, Sylvester Stallone, George Burns, Martin Scorsese, Richard Burton, François Truffaut, and Steven Spielberg. (And, yes, O. J. Simpson.) He's had dinner or lunch with the

Rolling Stones and Oliver Stone's mother (not at the same time). Then there was his era of regular television appearances on networks like CNN, CNBC, MSNBC, and Fox News, including shows (some of which leaned against his liberal convictions) like *The O'Reilly Factor*, *Scarborough Country*, *Countdown with Keith Olbermann*, *Hannity and Colmes*, and *Charlie Rose*.

His willingness to appear on such diverse programs is a sign of his considerate, open-minded way of being-in-the-world; unlike many critics, he is curious and receptive about the work of filmmakers and actors with politics very different from his own. In this respect, one of the things that has always struck me about David's criticism and reviews is how consistently generous he is (although he disagrees, stating, "I don't particularly think of myself as a generous or forgiving critic.") Not to say he is gullible or a soft touch, more that he is open to finding whatever redeeming elements he can in a work that others may find fatally flawed. This openness can even extend to the kinds of low-rent films many critics dismiss out of hand (apart from one movie—unnamed here—that he dismissed as "obscene gibberish").

Generosity goes hand-in-hand with modesty and an openness to admitting mistakes. David is happy to revise his earlier opinions on second or third viewings of movies that he did not fully appreciate the first time, or that he came to understand differently in retrospect. He is brave enough to criticize films by his favorite directors (such as John Cassavetes) if he finds them to be flawed. He also shows great generosity toward his critical colleagues, summarizing them as "judicious and congenial," even when he finds their opinions "weirdly off-base." Even outside the world of critics, although people may not agree with his opinions, nobody dislikes him (nobody I know of, at least).

It can be a little intimidating to interview someone well-known and respected for his own interview technique. David's relaxed, genial style has put many reputedly formidable celebrities at ease, and enabled him to develop special relationships with filmmakers like Truffaut and Cassavetes. Appropriately, he has edited interview anthologies on Jean-Luc Godard, Robert Altman, and Terry Gilliam. He is also, as people interested in his career will know, the author of books on Clint Eastwood, Spike Lee, Robert Altman, Alfred Hitchcock, and Godard, as well as three volumes on the Beat Generation, a long-standing interest of his (and the subject of his PhD dissertation). As he explains, he has always admired the "Beat ideal" of "changing human consciousness by way of challenging and undermining received forms of wisdom and behavior." In his writing, whether his readers are academics or casual moviegoers, David has an enviable facility for making difficult cinematic and philosophical ideas widely comprehensible.

David has always been a diligent—some might say obsessive—worker. During his New York years, he managed the spectacular feat of getting a PhD in his forties while teaching at Long Island University and working as the *Monitor* film critic. He was also, for many years, a member of the New York Film Festival selection committee and chair of the National Society of Film Critics and the New York Film Critics Circle. In addition, he wrote for a variety of publications, including *Film Comment*, *Film Quarterly* (which he edited for two years), *Quarterly Review of Film and Video* (which he edited for ten years), and many other publications.

When he turned 60, in 2005, David took a well-deserved early retirement from the *Monitor* and Long Island University, moving to Baltimore, where we have lived for the last twenty years. Even today, in his early eighties, David is as active as ever—he teaches multiple courses each semester at the Maryland Institute College of Art; he has a weekly radio show on an NPR affiliate (*Films in Focus* on Robin-HoodRadio); and he writes regularly for *Cineaste* magazine. He speaks at universities, attends international conferences, continues to be an avid opera, symphony, and theater goer, and still watches at least a movie a day. He regularly attends screenings at our local arthouse cinema (the Charles) but does not (always) turn up his nose at the multiplex. It is safe to say that his distinguished career is far from over. Characteristically, David is more modest and concise. "I keep watching and watching and watching, and every now and then the enterprise pays off."

Mikita Brottman is an author, professor, and psychoanalyst.

ACKNOWLEDGEMENTS

Many thanks to Paul Cronin for suggesting that I embark on this volume, which would never have come into being otherwise. Paul and I first met many a long year ago, and it's been a joy to work with him on what's turned out to be an enormous pleasure from start to finish. I owe equal gratitude to my amazing partner, Mikita Brottman, for her excellent questions, her unfailing humor, her good-natured skepticism, and her (almost) inexhaustible patience. Thanks as always to Jeremy and Craig, my brilliant and loving sons. And a very broad thank-you to the many critics, scholars, journalists, cinephiles, and friends who have been my companions during more than half a century of watching movies, going to the theater, listening to music, and sharing thoughts and feelings about all of it. It's been quite a trip, and many adventures are still to come.

PARADIGMS AND
PHILOSOPHIES

Let's start with a big question. Do you have a philosophy of film criticism?

Having a philosophy of criticism seems a little grand, but I have ideas that add up to an informal philosophy. One question that occasionally arises in this field is whether there's a distinction between critics and reviewers. A reasonable answer is that reviewers assume the reader may not have seen the film in question, so you should convey basic information about it while avoiding spoilers that give away the plot, whereas critics assume the reader is familiar with the movie and discuss it in more depth and detail than you'd find in a standard review. Reviewers and critics serve different but equally valid functions, as long as they're good at the trade, and within the two categories there's a pretty wide spectrum—at the extreme end of reviewing you find things like internet blogs, which may or may not be decently written and at least minimally intelligent, and at the extreme end of criticism you find the heavy varieties of academic analysis, which may or may not be clearly written and at least minimally understandable by people who aren't specialists in cinema studies.

Whatever the venue is, I think the critic's opinion of a film—did I like it, did I hate it, did it make me laugh or cry or get hungry or want to get the hell out—is far less important than the information I convey *about* the film. This will include a rundown of the plot, naturally, and depending on the movie being reviewed it may also involve historical or cultural context, or background on how and why the production was made, or facts about the director and actors and other creative personnel, or anything else that seems germane. Even if I strongly signal that I like or dislike the film, readers should be given enough information to form their own provisional opinions, which may go in the opposite direction: Sterritt loved it but I can tell from his review that I'd hate it, or Sterritt hated it but his review makes me think I'd love it. My bottom-line yea or nay matters, but it's not what matters most in the review.

Beyond that, my personal crusade has been to encourage more *adventurous* moviegoing. Even casual moviegoers have much to gain by looking beyond Hollywood hits and giving a shot to challenging art films, productions from the silent era, films from far-flung countries, and avant-garde works that require active thinking by the viewer. Cinema is a vast and varied artform. Let a zillion flowers bloom!

*In your writing, do you distinguish between the usual terms—
"cinema," "film," and "movie"—for the artform itself?*

Two more, "motion picture" and "moving picture," are
also pretty common. I generally use them interchangeably,
although "movie" seems the most informal and "cinema"
has a more high-toned ring, at least for American readers.
They all mean the same thing. I'm not fussy about this.

*Is it possible for you to summarize the most important thing
or things you look for in a film? Are there basic qualities that
separate the good ones from the bad ones?*

There are no formulas or checklists, that's for sure. Solid
work on the level of craft seems like a basic requirement, but
there are some relatively roughshod pictures that make up in
inspiration or energy what they lack in polish or filmmaking
expertise. Then too, avant-garde films have to be judged by
standards very different from those of mainstream narrative movies, and those standards also vary greatly among
different experimental filmmakers. Of course I like movies
that succeed on the level of plain entertainment value, with
no lofty intellectual or aesthetic pretensions, but only the
best of them live very long in my memory. The very best
films combine the things I just mentioned—intelligence,
artistic worth and originality, themes and ambience that are
absorbing and thought-provoking or at least entertaining
and fun—as well as some kind of engaging *je ne sais quoi*, to
fall back on a handy cliché.

And there's another thing I'll indulge myself by
mentioning: a sense of mystery, which is something I value
in all areas of art and life. This goes back a long way with
me. When a college friend told me the thing he wanted most
in life was romance, it occurred to me that as important as
romance certainly is, I wanted something more, something
that's all the more desirable because it exceeds my ability
to say exactly what it is. I suppose this explains why I'm
not generally fond of the whodunit genre, which is all about
explaining and dispelling mystery, and it surely explains my
deep affection for the likes of Tarkovsky and Sokurov and
Bresson and Brakhage and other screen artists who don't
make easily spelled-out meanings a high priority. Their
films tend toward the mysterious and ineffable and unde-
finable, qualities that defy precise expression but have enormous power on the screen. Those are the films that ultimately matter most to me.

Outlets

Before we continue in this vein, can you tell me what publications you've written for and edited over the years?

My main outlet was *The Christian Science Monitor*. I started there with a nonwriting job in 1967, before I had quite finished college, and about a year later I officially became a staff writer and critic. Except for a brief period around 1970, when I left to become editor of the weekly *Boston After Dark*, I was at the *Monitor* straight through to 2005, when I took early retirement.

And other publications?

I need to look at a list to answer this. The higher-profile venues include *The New York Times*, *The Chronicle of Higher Education*, *PopMatters*, *Huffington Post*, *IndieWire*, and the jazz magazine *DownBeat*. Outside the United States there's been the legendary French magazine *Cahiers du cinéma*, the strangely named Austrian periodical *Blimp*, and the fine Canadian publication *Cinema Scope*. Other outlets have included *Senses of Cinema*, *Movie*, *Movie-Maker*, *Framework*, *Film International*, *Film/Philosophy*, *Undercurrent*, *Moving Image Source*, published by the American Museum of the Moving Image, *IFCRant*, *Facets Multi-Media*, and the *New Review of Television Studies*. Also some periodicals with interests beyond movies—the *Journal of the American Psychoanalytic Association*, *The Journal of American History*, *Western American Literature*, *Mosaic*, *CounterPunch*, which specializes in politics, *Beliefnet*, which deals with religious matters, *Sexuality and Culture*, *Stagebill*, and the *Journal of French and Francophone Philosophy*. Plus articles for three journals—*Cinema Journal*, the *Journal of Beat Studies*, and the *Hitchcock Annual*—where I've served on the editorial boards. At certain points I also wrote regularly for *Tikkun* and *Islands*, where I was film critic and video critic, respectively.

And editing?

I was co-editor of my high-school paper—the other co-editor later became the Ideas and Viewpoints editor at *Newsday*—but that was ages and ages ago! More to the point, I was the editor of *Boston After Dark* in my youth and more recently of *Quarterly Review of Film and Video*, a journal from Taylor & Francis and Routledge, two big outfits in the journal field. And for a couple of years I was guest editor of *Film Quarterly*, a University of California Press publication. I didn't want that job permanently, but I agreed to do it temporarily after the previous editor, Rob White, disappeared from the position—nowadays we'd say he ghosted it—without a moment's notice, greatly discombobulating the folks in the publisher's office.

And speaking?

Leaving out any number of cinema clubs and classrooms, I've lectured at the National Gallery of Art, the Museum of Modern Art, the Brooklyn Museum, the Boston Museum of Fine Arts, the Motion Picture Association of America, and various other places.

Much activity!

Too much activity!

Auteurism

Now back to major issues in film criticism. What's your take on auteur theory? Has it been a good paradigm or a bad one for film culture?

Auteurism is certainly a big issue in movie criticism, where it has a lot of practical importance, and also in film theory. I first ran across the concept in film magazines when I was beginning to take a serious interest in cinema, and it took me a little while to figure out just what it was and how it worked. Like my colleague Andrew Sarris, who played a key role in importing the idea from French criticism to American criticism, I saw what a good tool it is for organizing film history. And for teasing out the personal, idiosyncratic resonances nested in the enterprise of crafting narrative movies, which is a largely impersonal process driven by technology and drenched in the lust for profits. It was easy to detect the personalities of my early favorites— Truffaut, Godard, Bergman, Fellini, et al—in the pictures they made, and it wasn't hard to learn the stylistic signatures of Hollywood giants like Chaplin, Sternberg, Hitchcock, Ford, and so on

Before long I got beyond the basics and started thinking of movies—good movies, and sometimes not-so-good ones—as products of both individual artistry and what the great André Bazin called the genius of the system. I largely agree with the auteurist idea that different directors using the same screenplay may emerge with very different movies. A standard example is what might happen with the Little Red Riding Hood story. One director might concentrate the visuals on the little girl, making a story of threatened innocence; another director might concentrate mainly on the wolf, creating a study of evil; and a third might keep the camera at a distance, emphasizing the physical placements of the characters and making an action picture. That makes sense to me.

Auteur theory has flaws and limitations, to be sure. It certainly oversimplifies the ways in which films are made, understating or obscuring the contributions of cinematographers, art directors, and editors, not to mention screenwriters and actors. No less an inventor of auteurism than Jean-Luc Godard eventually admitted the oversimplification problem, and he started pointing to the key role played by producers, often seen as mere money-mongers by people outside the industry. Then too, Sarris's book *The American Cinema* has influenced my generation of critics more than any other single work, and his rankings—with labels like The Pantheon, The Far Side of Paradise, Lightly Likable, Strained Seriousness, and so on—have been skewing critical tastes ever since the book appeared in the late '60s.

Of course an enormous number of talents have arisen since Andrew's rankings came out, and many overlooked talents have been uncovered and reassessed, but auteurism has been overused here as well, with critics grabbing any sign of stylistic consistency as a marker of directorial uniqueness rather than, say, lazy repetition or failure of imagination. That kind of study can be interesting, but the results can be less than persuasive. I also have an auteurist friend who believes that the work of a great director steadily deepens as the director gathers wisdom and maturity with the passage of years. This sort of thinking leads to the overvaluation of, say, Ford's late *7 Women*, and Hawks's *Man's Favorite Sport?* and *Red Line 7000*, and Hitchcock's *Torn Curtain* and *Topaz*—all movies with some merit, but hardly on the same plane as earlier masterworks by those directors. And it fails to explain how, for instance, Lindsay Anderson could go from the power of *This Sporting Life* in 1963 to the clunkiness of *The Whales of August* in 1987.

There's also the category I've named the "clear-blue-sky movie," which is a film that seems to come out of the blue, taking me by surprise because it's an excellent picture by a director whose work normally turns me off. Richard Attenborough's *Shadowlands*, about the great author C. S. Lewis and his wife, is an example. It's always a bit sad when an excellent director makes a disappointing movie, but it's nice when things go the other way.

Can people other than directors be auteurs?

Absolutely. A film adaptation of a Shakespeare play could be directed with no particular style but still be effective through its acting and the text itself, in which case Shakespeare and/ or the actors would be the primary creative forces, i.e. the auteurs of the movie. For another, a Marx Brothers movie is a Marx Brothers movie no matter who wrote and directed it, even when major talents like Leo McCarey or S. J. Perelman were on the creative team.

There's also the interesting case of Walt Disney and company. He started as the creator and mastermind of ingenious animations, a genuine auteur with original ideas and plenty of talent for putting them on the screen. When his enterprise expanded from short animations to feature-length cartoons, live-action movies, and television shows, vastly more creative contributors had to be involved, but Disney's stamp—some aspects of style and a general insistence on family-friendly content—was still very much there. It wasn't until some twenty years after his death that the company released a movie without a G rating—*The Black Cauldron* was a PG picture—and then moved into a whole range of content that wasn't aimed at kids or even suitable for them, becoming a regular production company while still exploiting the Disney name for its family-oriented material.

I've written about the Disney operation countless times, and I've interviewed major players like the great Disney animators Frank Thomas and Ollie Johnston and the founder's brother, Roy Disney, who resembled his sibling in looks and in his addiction to cigarettes. It's hardly one of my more ambitious essays, but I enjoyed writing a Turner Classic Movies piece on *The Living Desert*, a 1953 documentary marketed under the True-Life Adventures banner, a line Disney had started in 1948, winning multiple Academy Awards in the then-extant category of best two-reel short. *The Living Desert* was the first feature-length entry in the series, inspired by footage of a battle between a beetle and a tarantula sent to Disney by a grad student who then did much of the movie's camerawork. I'll quote a bit of that article:

> [A] wildlife documentary like *The Living Desert* has to deal with sex and death—not two of Disney's

strongest areas, to state the obvious. The narrator alludes to death quite early, saying that the desert embodies "the ancient drama of the struggle for existence, and for the most part, life here is a bit on the grim side." He quickly adds that "there's always comedy relief," and the sight of a hopping roadrunner bears out the point. Still, you can't get around the fact that desert animals stay alive by eating other desert animals. The film's main response is denial. It displays a fair amount of chasing and stalking, but nothing larger than a millipede gets gobbled on camera, and the confrontations between predator and prey—a rattlesnake and a hawk, for instance—generally end with the latter reaching safety in the nick of time...

The film gives more time to sex, or rather to courtship patterns and mating displays, accompanied by the narrator's most brazenly anthropomorphic language and the soundtrack's most shamelessly tricked-up music. The low point comes when the wooing behavior of two scorpions is played as a square dance complete with romping fiddles and calls of "allemande left" and "do sa do." Audiences were willing to swallow this in 1953, but today the average eight-year-old will find it too cutesy for comfort.

Its demerits notwithstanding, *The Living Desert* earned one of the four Oscars accrued by Disney for 1953, a record for the most won by one person in one year, and it earned $5 million in its first release against a production cost of just $300,000. It also got awards at the Cannes and Berlin festivals. And it sparked a big change in the Disney setup. The company's usual distributor, RKO, was antsy about documentaries, and disagreements about *The Living Desert* induced Disney to start his own Buena Vista Distribution branch, another resounding success. I have no particular affection for *The Living Desert*, but poking into its history was fun.

And on the topic of documentaries, it bears mentioning that some non-fiction filmmakers are good candidates for auteur status, even though their task is recording and structuring material from the real world rather than crafting fictional worlds cooked up by their imaginations. Even the documentary-shy Sarris regarded Robert Flaherty as an auteur, and I'd certainly place Errol Morris, Frederick Wiseman, Michael Moore, and a few others into the category. Film scholar Joe McElhaney wrote a book on the Maysles Brothers as auteurs. That notion goes against the grain, since Al and David worked with numerous collaborators and often made sponsored films, but Joe makes a persuasive case.

Can television directors be auteurs?

Television used to be described as a producer's medium, not a director's medium, but the dividing lines aren't always clearcut. Hitchcock, for instance, was the presiding spirit of his TV show, *Alfred Hitchcock Presents*, and although he personally directed only a few episodes, some of those have his distinctive stamp. Today television belongs to the showrunners who get the "created by" credits. Some of them certainly have distinctive styles, and I'm happy to regard the best ones as televisual auteurs.

Critical opinions

I have the feeling that you tend to be generous in your opinions as a critic. Do you try to find something nice to say about a film even if it's rubbish?

Hmm... I don't particularly think of myself as a generous or forgiving critic, but I suppose it's relatively rare to find a movie that's totally awful in every way, so I'll probably try to mention whatever glimmer of light manages to make its way into a generally rotten picture. I remember dismissing a horror film I hated as "obscene gibberish," so I can be pretty unsparing when I'm sufficiently riled up.

Have you ever been attacked for a negative review, either by angry viewers or angry filmmakers?

Sure. I discovered long ago that the angriest reactions often come from people who don't have an opposite opinion from mine, but who really love a movie and are upset that I didn't like it *enough*, that I didn't swoon for it as much as they did. It's an odd phenomenon.

And people working in the commercial film industry can suffer from, oh, let's call it a lack of perspective. After I gave a so-so review to a new film on NPR, someone phoned to ask me if I knew how hard it is to make a movie, informing me that everyone who gets a movie onto the screen should get an Academy Award for that alone! Seems to me those Oscar ceremonies would go on for days and days.

In any case, the critic's job is to have a dialogue with moviegoers on one hand and moviemakers on the other, and the dialogue isn't very helpful if the critic is relentlessly upbeat. The trite old phrase "constructive criticism" is still worth bearing in mind.

You must have given unfavorable reviews to movies made by people you know personally. What's that like for you, and have any of those people expressed anger toward you?

A television critic I knew told me that if stating a negative opinion means upsetting a friend, he chooses the friend over the opinion. Not me! But I admit I may try to soften the blow a bit by using measured language. Spalding Gray was a good friend, and I admired many of the monologues that made him famous. But eventually they lost the spontaneity they'd had in the beginning, and when I wrote that he was in danger of becoming a mere sit-down comedian, he wasn't bothered at all. Nor was I bothered when he pretty much ignored my warning! At one point he tried to recapture some of the spontaneity by having a second performer onstage with him, starting him off with a randomly chosen word and cutting him off after an arbitrary amount of time. I thought this was a mistake, weakening the monologue's effect, and I phoned to tell him what my review would say, adding that my negative words would bolster my overall credibility about his work by assuring readers that I didn't automatically like everything he did. He agreed, and he mentioned a *Village Voice* critic who *did* automatically like everything he did. So we saw eye to eye on this.

There have been cases where an artist has really cared about my point of view and reacted badly when I've expressed disappointment. I got to know the very great playwright and screenwriter Horton Foote pretty well, and once when he sent me a VHS cassette of his latest film, I simply didn't have time to watch it right away, and I think that bothered him. Then his play *The Young Man from Atlanta* opened on Broadway, and in my *Monitor* review I gave him a lavish dose of well-deserved praise but said that the lead performances by Rip Torn and Shirley Knight needed more psychological deepening and that the dialogue was sometimes rambling and repetitious. I never heard from Horton again.

Another case is Robert Duvall, a superb actor, and one who worked quite a bit with Horton, by the way. I got to know Duvall when he wrote and directed the badly underrated film *Angelo My Love*, which I loved. Several years later he starred in *Convicts*, a small independent movie written by Horton, and I wrote that while Duvall is one of the greatest American actors ever to grace the screen or stage, he isn't at his absolute best in this particular film. And he fired off a handwritten letter so angry you could almost see the penpoint tearing through the paper! A few years later I wanted to interview him about *The Apostle*, another very good film he wrote and directed, and the publicist said it wouldn't happen because Bob was upset about my *Convicts* review—he'd evidently been brooding about that for half a dozen years. I said Bob should take another look at that review, which was anything but a hatchet job, and whether or not he actually did that, he changed his mind and agreed to the interview, which went pleasantly and smoothly. It's nice to know that an actor and filmmaker of Duvall's stature has taken my opinions so seriously, but it seems to me that an actor and filmmaker of that stature doesn't have to be so touchy.

Are there times when you've changed your opinion of a film in a major way after going on record with your original view?

Yep, it happens. A major shift or reversal of opinion doesn't happen often, but my response to a film on a second or third or umpteenth viewing is usually a bit different from the way I felt on the first viewing, and occasionally it's very different. I first saw *The Shining* at a critics' screening, and it seemed somewhat chilly to me, rather distant and certainly not as horrifying as a first-rate horror movie should be. I was talking with Brian De Palma not long after the screening, and I gave him the opinion I just gave you, and he was very interested because he hadn't seen the picture yet. Later it turned out that Stephen King had a similar view, as he told me when I interviewed him.

The next time I saw *The Shining* the circumstances were the opposite of ideal—it was in the ramshackle screening room where I taught most of my Long Island University classes, drastically more downscale than the place where I'd seen it earlier. And from the first moments I was blown away by it. The traveling shots at the beginning transfixed me, and I stayed transfixed right to the end. How could I have been so thickheaded the first time I saw it? My theory is that I'd recently read King's novel for the first time and it was very present in my mind, interfering in some strange way with my perceptions of the film as it unfolded. But that's no excuse. I was thickheaded, period. In dramatic, cinematic, and narrative terms *The Shining* is a magisterial achievement, as many subsequent viewings have amply confirmed.

And so it goes with other movies from time to time. Sometimes a radical upgrading is in order, as with *The Shining*, and sometimes I go the other way, downgrading a picture I'd overrated earlier. And sometimes my opinion remains quite steady. As much as I respect most of Kubrick's films, for instance, I didn't much like *A Clockwork Orange* in 1971 and subsequent viewings haven't changed my mind. Of course, I'm not alone in having occasional swerves in my critical opinions. For one example, I was on the selection committee when Scorsese submitted *The Last Temptation of Christ* to the New York Film Festival, and I saw multiple problems with it—some clunky acting, a few jangling accents, inconsistencies of tone and style. But my colleague Phillip Lopate thought it was terrific. Later he backtracked and lowered his opinion, expressing surprise that the movie's flaws hadn't struck him harder the first time around. I could have told him, and I probably did. For another example from my NYFF days, Stuart Klawans was hugely enthusiastic about Michael Haneke's purposefully morbid *Benny's Video*, so in a conversation years later I was surprised when he inveighed against Haneke's work as a whole—he now believed Haneke was "dumb." I disagree, but Stuart is a first-rate critic, and someday I may come around to his view. Probably not, though.

Industry views

Do you find that filmmakers, actors, and others in the film industry are generally authoritative in their views on film? Or are they just one set of voices among many, despite their first-hand experience?

It's an interesting question. Their direct involvement in moviemaking obviously gives them a degree of expertise in their own areas of activity and whatever other areas they've been in a position to observe. Then again, it's a truism that the fresh eye of an outside observer can reveal things the insiders miss. I've learned a lot from asking directors and actors about how and why they do the things they do, but in matters of judgment and opinion my own views are just as valid. That's what makes a critic a critic.

And comments by people in the industry can be as misguided or irrelevant as comments by outsiders. I recall a period in the late '60s and early '70s when censorship was drastically diminishing and a lot of Hollywood insiders—

aging Hollywood insiders—were as disgruntled about the loosening standards as the worst squares in the audience, and I sometimes got little lectures on the topic from people I interviewed. For an example I looked up my 1979 interview with Stanley Kramer, a director and producer with a raging social conscience and a filmography ranging from the heights to the depths, with commendably progressive items like *The Defiant Ones*, *On the Beach*, *Inherit the Wind*, and *Judgment at Nuremberg*, and misfires like *The Runner Stumbles*, which ended his career in 1979. You might think he'd welcome the move away from Production Code prudery, but here's some of what he said to me: "Some people seem to think that dropping censorship makes you daring, but it doesn't. Just because you're allowed to show sex and bathrooms on screen, for realism, doesn't mean you have to do it! Certain things are private, and I prefer not to show them. But we've become a nation of watchers. We don't want to do any more; we want to watch other people do things for us." The last point makes a certain amount of sense, although I personally plan to keep having my own sex and going to my own bathroom, but Stanley's complaint about bodily functions is the sort of thing we heard a lot in that era. Since then times have fortunately changed.

To be fair to Kramer, many of his films were genuinely important in their day, and his steadfast Hollywood liberalism was admirable. And he ended my 1979 interview with a refreshing comment: "A few years ago I was at Stanford giving a talk. I said I'd been fighting the establishment for 35 years, and I still don't know what the establishment is. A student got up and called out, 'Maybe because it's you!' And you know, that could be very true. Very true." I wish all filmmakers had their careers so clearly in perspective.

Do your interests in different artforms merge and relate to each other? In other words, do you write and think about film, music, literature, opera, art, and so on in different ways, or do you have an approach or style that applies across the board—sort of a theory of everything?

I suppose my style is pretty much the same, aside from the different kinds of language appropriate to different venues—reviews in a newspaper, review essays in a specialist magazine, academic essays in a scholarly journal. My main goal is to stay as clear and communicative as the material and my probable audience allow. It's not a complicated agenda.

Do you take notes when watching a film you'll be reviewing?

Pretty much never. You can miss things when you take your eyes off the screen, and I regret to report that writing in the dark is a skill I've never fully mastered. I may jot some notes when I watch something on video, using the pause button, but not in a theater or screening room. I watch the movie as attentively as I can and write any necessary notes when it's over. But that's a personal choice, and some critics operate differently. We all have our own methods and habits.

Do you ever watch a film more than once before writing about it?

It varies. When you're reviewing for a daily newspaper, you usually get one shot at the movie before your deadline, but when you're writing an in-depth critical analysis you may see a film many, many times over months or years. For serious writing about serious films, multiple viewings are highly desirable and even mandatory. I don't share Pauline Kael's insistence on seeing a movie just once before banging out a review. She was an entertaining and influential writer, but her work might have been deeper and smarter if she hadn't adopted that peculiar principle.

When you start a new article or essay, do you outline it in advance? Do you know how it will proceed and how it will finish?

I don't make an outline, and although I certainly start with an idea or two or three, sometimes I'm quite surprised by how things turn out in the end. Occasionally I'm even startled. One example is an essay I wrote for the *Hitchcock Annual* back when Christopher Brookhouse was the editor there. What interested me at the start was how many indirect references Hitchcock's last completed film, *Family Plot*, made to many of Hitch's earlier films—a pretty basic notion, and I wasn't sure how I'd develop it.

As I started writing, I got interested in the many varieties of ambiguity that play large parts in Hitchcock's work, which is one reason for the endless amounts of interpretation his movies invite, as demonstrated by the extremely wide bookshelf of Hitchcock studies. From there I started thinking more broadly about the last stages of his career, when both his filmography and his life were approaching their inevitable end, and that led me to ideas drawn from Michel Chion's work on cinematic sound and Slavoj Žižek's rambunctious use of Jacques Lacan's psychoanalytic theories. And while I'm not a religious person, I have a longtime fascination with religion as an area of human thought and culture, and Hitchcock occasionally spoke of his Roman Catholic background, which he never left entirely behind. Much like *Family Plot* itself, I found myself referring to various earlier films, from *The Lodger* and *The 39 Steps* to *I Confess* and *Psycho*. I ended up with an essay very different from what I'd expected, but it evidently worked, since Chris made it the lead essay in the new issue and Sid Gottlieb included it in his collection of selected pieces from the *Annual*. Leaving aside the quality of the essay, which may or may not be as high as my editors felt at the time, seeing how it evolved made me realize that academic writing—interpretive writing, not straightforward research or film-historical writing—can be a genuinely creative enterprise.

Can you say a bit more about your interest in religion?

Particular religious dogmas and preachments generally strike me as implausible or crazy, but going into the more sophisticated theological ideas is a way of opening up thought beyond the confines of the everyday world in which we're almost always trapped, mentally as well as physically. That's as close as I can come to describing why I periodically return to it as a subject.

When you're writing about a film made in the past, is its historical context an important factor?

Historical, cultural, and social contexts are always pertinent, although there's no strict rule about how much or how often they enter a particular article or essay. I'll take this opportunity to mention a habit of some critics that has always bugged me—the way they have of making a point sound ultra-important by claiming that *this or that* is the "most *this or that* in the history of the cinema." While that's a valid thing to say in some limited areas, when the *this or that* is actually rare or unique, it's extremely pretentious in most circumstances, suggesting that you know the whole history of cinema well enough to make such a sweeping pronouncement. And that's the case even though the history of the cinema isn't that long! Projected motion pictures weren't invented until the 1890s, and the whole span of their existence is the blink of an eye compared with that of music or painting or any other artform. So for me this is a formulation to avoid.

A practical question: where do screenings for critics take place? In theaters or other locations?

It varies. There are a number of private screening rooms in New York, basically little theaters with relatively small screens and reasonably comfortable seats, depending on the venue. For big Hollywood releases the studios and distributors often book an auditorium in a regular theater and mark off a few rows for critics and other privileged personages. Those are sometimes known as "cattle call" screenings, and they pose more danger of putting you near people who talk or munch popcorn or, God help us, sneak in a phone call. I've always preferred screening rooms to theaters, although the large theatrical screen can be a plus.

Does it bother you when people talk during a film?

I wouldn't say it bothers me, I'd say it bothers me a great deal! Movies demand the respect of quiet, undisturbed surroundings, at least for critics who'll be opining and passing judgment on them. That means no talking, no coming and going. Laughter is all right as long as it's a comedy or a comic moment. But no noisy eating, please! And no unwrapping crinkly packaging! If you desperately need to get a wrapper off, don't try to do it slowly, which makes for more prolonged noise—just rend the air asunder with one mighty rip and get it over with!

Here's a very practical question—have you ever gotten stiff from sitting in screening-room seats for hours at a stretch?

Never more than I could handle, although I don't have the world's most limber lower back. But in my days as a newspaper critic and festival programmer, I was very aware of how remarkably sedentary the life of a reviewer can be—someone once remarked that critics are professional spectators, and that rings somewhat true. Then again, we're also professional writers, and while the writing sessions also involve sitting for long periods, poking the keyboard takes at least a little effort. In any case, I saw the hazards of a sedentary career, and for many years I ran five miles a day as a way of keeping my body in some sort of shape. And during the decades when I lived on lower Broadway I had a rule about walking, not taking cabs or the subway, to any screening or appointment in Tribeca or Soho, which were south for most Manhattanites but north for me.

Another topic: you've written countless words about movies, but have you ever been in *the movies?*

In the most modest ways imaginable. I play a film scholar based on me in a horror movie called *Butterfly Kisses*, written and directed by Erik Kristopher Myers in 2018. It's about an urban legend and a box of mysterious videocassettes, and my character is an expert who may be able to cast light on the mystery. Not a great work of cinema, but I performed my sequences in the comfort of my apartment, and Erik was fun to work with. I appear in a party scene in *Garbo Talks*, a minor Sidney Lumet picture, and I'm in Paul Cronin's documentary *"Look out Haskell, it's real!,"* about the making of Haskell Wexler's film *Medium Cool*. I'm also in numerous DVD extras, talking about Hitchcock and Godard, and I've done some audio commentaries too. But my performing has taken place mainly in the classroom, not on the big screen.

ORIGINS

Now let's go back to the beginning. What were the early movies in your life?

My parents liked movies, so as a kid I went to the movies a lot, to the point where I got tired of it at certain points along the way. But it was an activity I enjoyed, and while many movies bored me, others were a lot of fun. I'm not sure of this, but I think the first movie I ever saw might have been a Disney picture called *So Dear to My Heart*, which is a partly live-action, partly animated movie about a little boy who has a pet lamb. One of the people in that movie is Burl Ives, whom I interviewed many decades later, so when I think something is done with in my life it may come around in a different form many years later. I looked at that movie again as an adult and wasn't all that impressed by it, but as what might have been my first movie, way back in the early 1950s, it's just slightly dear to my heart.

My saga really started with radio and television, though. As a very young kid, before TV had spread its tentacles throughout American life, I heard radio shows like *Sky King*, about an airplane-flying rancher of that name, and *Our Miss Brooks*, with Eve Arden as a likable schoolteacher, and *Sergeant Preston of the Yukon*, which implanted its theme song, poached from an opera by Emil von Reznicek, permanently in my brain.

In my teenage years I was a rock'n'roll fanatic addicted to top-40 radio, and I listened intently to Alan Freed's pioneering show, which played rhythm-and-blues records by Black artists who were otherwise hard to hear; the racial angle didn't mean much to me as a young kid, but the music was self-evidently excellent. I also listened to disc jockeys like Irv Smith, better known as A Smith Named Irv, who died in a car accident on the way to the studio one day, and Murray Kaufman, who started calling himself Murray the K and became a leading deejay of the era. And I was very interested when disc jockey Peter Tripp, who nicknamed himself The Curly-Headed Kid in the Third Row, did his famous publicity stunt of staying awake for just over 200 hours, apparently helped by uppers near the end, and broadcasting all the while, his speech increasingly slurred but still reasonably coherent. The careers of Freed and Tripp were scuttled by the 1960 payola scandal, in which various radio personalities were convicted of taking bribes to play particular records. This was just a few years after some of the big quiz shows scandalized America by secretly rigging the outcomes for telegenic contestants, so it was a boom time for media chicanery.

I also have to mention Jean Shepherd, whose WOR radio show—aimed at "night people," as he called them—seemed amazingly cool to me and some of my friends. He mainly spun anecdotes about his life and times, most or all of them probably invented, and sometimes he'd play along with some record on a kazoo, which seemed silly to me even then. I was taken aback when I discovered that my somewhat square brother and hopelessly square grandmother had become fans of his radio show—it seems that not all the night people were noticeably hip—but he retained a warm little spot in my heart. Shepherd later achieved well-deserved acclaim for writing and narrating the utterly delightful film *A Christmas Story*, which extended his radio monologues into the movie realm. I also saw him perform live in New York in the late '60s or early '70s, and his act was as good as the radio show. He was a genuine artiste of the audio airwaves, along with such notables as Stan Freberg and the team of Bob and Ray.

One of my early visual enthusiasms was the View-Master viewer, a plastic gizmo with two eyepieces; you looked at twinned pictures mounted on a circular piece of cardboard inserted into the viewer, providing marvelous 3D effects and terrific color. There were seven image pairs on each "reel." Some reels told a brief story with puppet characters, but the ones that pleased me most were nature scenes—mountains, rivers, and the like. I've never been a big nature buff, but the rich colors and vivid depth effects of these reels unquestionably influenced my aesthetics for decades to come. They made a strong and lasting impression on me.

Records, of the old-fashioned 78 rpm variety, were also a presence in my early life. I envied the kid next door because he had a radio, which offered vastly more variety than my little record player and little record collection, but I can still conjure memories of *Bozo Under the Sea*, which came with a picture book and instructions to turn the page each time Bozo made a bubble sound with his diving gear. I can still sing small snatches of the music on the *Alice in Wonderland* recording by Fred Waring and His Pennsylvanians, although some of that album's storytelling was confusing to my little-boy mind. I also liked *Peter and the Wolf*, narrated by the reliably marvelous Boris Karloff, and *Tubby the Tuba*, with its comic musical character. Good stuff.

In elementary school I played violin and clarinet, wretchedly I'm sure, and in high school I played French horn, a little less wretchedly I hope. I was in the concert band and the marching band, where I acquired one of my more surprising tastes, a lasting love for the great Sousa marches. All the while I took piano lessons, and playing in the high-school dance band was quite an experience. There happened to be several marvelously musical kids in the class just ahead of me—some of them went on to college for music—and in rehearsals I'd sit at the piano, do a mediocre job on my own parts, and listen to the others knock out sensational solos and ensemble work. I've loved swing jazz ever since. Eventually I also took organ lessons, and I was a professional church organist for a few years. So music has been with me forever.

Television

Say more about your history with television.

I was born in 1944, so I was in the first-ever TV generation. I'm not sure how accurate this memory is, but I seem to remember my parents getting our first TV set when I was about seven years old, which would have been about 1951 or '52. Some other families on the block already had one—we lived in a modest Long Island neighborhood—but ours had a respectable seventeen-inch screen, considerably bigger than the tiny model our next-door neighbors had.

I have vague memories of shows from that era. There were staples like *The Howdy Doody Show* and *The Gabby Hayes Show* and *Winky-Dink and You*, which invited kids to stick a piece of transparent plastic on the screen and interact with the show by drawing on it—very postmodern, but not ideal for someone as bad at drawing as I was. *Captain Video and His Video Rangers*, an aptly titled science-fiction epic, was a favorite of mine. A little later there were *The Adventures of Superman*, sitcoms like *I Married Joan*, with Joan Davis and Jim Backus, and *My Little Margie*, with Gale Storm and Charles Farrell, and adventure shows like *The Lone Ranger* and *The Adventures of Rin Tin Tin*, and the ever-popular Walt Disney shows, *Disneyland* and *The Mickey Mouse Club*. I'd watch TV with my parents or my younger brother or by myself. We wouldn't exactly analyze the shows and movies, but we'd talk about the jokes and adventure scenes we liked. I make no claims for the quality of these programs, but all were extremely popular in their day. The baby boomers were a growing audience, and although I was born slightly before the postwar surge, I benefited—or suffered, maybe—from the upswell of kid-oriented programming.

And some of it was pretty good. I have a relatively clear memory of a skit I saw on one of the children's shows, and while I can't remember what show it was, the fact that I've always remembered it is a sign of how far back my interest in moving images evidently goes. The show's main character used a sort of two-way TV to have conversations with someone on another planet, and I'll paraphrase the episode that has stayed with me. The other-planet person is looking at a straight vertical line, which wiggles and shimmies a bit, and he says, "That was an interesting twist." The earthbound man asks how seeing such an ordinary thing could be enjoyable—don't people on your planet have movies like we do? We used to have your kind of movies, the space person replies, but this kind is much safer. For a long time we had 2D movies, and then we started making 3D movies. Then we invented 4D movies, where you could taste and smell everything on the screen. Next we invented 5D movies, where you could *feel* everything on the screen. And then we invented 6D movies, where everything in the movie actually *happened* to the people in the audience. Only one 6D movie was ever made—it was called *The Big Explosion*! And then we decided to stay with 1D movies—like I said, they're much safer.

That still tickles me. Quite a witty take on cultural and technological progress!

What did your family think of movies? Did you watch movies on television with them?

My parents took me to the movies fairly often, although they were very conservative about what I was allowed to see. We also watched a lot of television together, and I watched a lot of TV on my own. I was fascinated by it. My parents were very bright, but they weren't intellectuals—my stepfather worked in a bank and my mother was what used to be called a housewife—and when it came to entertainment we were an ordinary middle-class American family of the time. I'm not sure why, but we seemed to watch a lot of Charlie Chan movies on TV. Maybe I remember that because whodunits have never been one of my favorite genres and my aversion to them was probably forming around then.

Do you ever think about those childhood TV and radio experiences when you're dealing with current film and television?

Once in a while, I suppose, but certainly not often. Then again, some of those ancient things can come to mind at unexpected moments. Not long ago I was revisiting a fine

MGM musical of the middle '50s, *It's Always Fair Weather*, and my ears perked up when a minor character started speaking near the end. The actor was Willard Waterman, who'd starred in *The Great Gildersleeve*, a TV show I'd seen around the time that movie was being made. I don't remember much else from that long-gone and surely mediocre sitcom, but Waterman had a distinctive voice, and it appears to be lodged in a few of my brain cells.

More to the point, some of my early TV experiences played into interests I was developing elsewhere. I did a lot of reading in science-fiction and fantasy magazines, for instance, and '50s and early-'60s shows like *Science Fiction Theatre* and *Twilight Zone* and the Roald Dahl series *Way Out*, which was surprisingly tough-minded, helped fuel my ongoing curiosity about those genres. I was also curious about things my parents regarded as too morbid for kids, so I naturally veered in that direction, seeing whatever horror movies I could get to, very much including the movies broadcast on *Shock Theater*, which was hosted by the amusing Zacherley in what passed for that show's golden age. I also liked the magazine *Famous Monsters of Filmland*, which once printed a letter I wrote about something or other. The magazine misspelled my last name, for which my awful handwriting was surely to blame.

These experiences are worth mentioning because they must have played a part in shaping the tastes, interests, and proclivities that have steered my cultural appetites, and influenced my work as a critic, ever since. I still see a lot of horror movies, for example, although that's partly because they're a hugely prolific genre nowadays. Then again, even the most glowingly reviewed ones usually turn out to be negligible or worse, and I keep meaning to swear off them or at least become super-selective about which ones to check out. What I really need to do is finish growing up, I suppose.

Getting serious

Tell me when you first realized you had a serious interest in film.

There's no one particular moment. I didn't take movies very seriously as a child, because they were something that everyone just did. They were a few blocks away and you went to see them and that was that. What I did take seriously as a kid was reading, and also theater. I think my family situation had something to do with my interest in theater. I was fascinated by the idea of role-playing, the idea that you could appear to be one way on the outside when in fact you were quite different inside yourself. So a strategy for living was to keep up the façade that affects how other people perceive you. When I was in elementary school, my favorite book in the school library was a book of one-act plays for children, and I would read the plays and imagine I was playing roles, trying on various personas. I also remember some slightly older kids in school putting on a play about a man who attends his own funeral and hears what everyone says about him; at the climax he hears the voices again, played for the audience on a backstage tape recorder, and the recording speeds up until it turns to gibberish, mimicking the psychological impact of the voices on the poor guy. That made a big impression on me, and its unconventional aspects—the repeated voices, the distorted sound—anticipated my longstanding interest in experimental and avant-garde performance.

As I got older, I graduated to other kinds of plays, although I didn't have a chance to actually see a whole lot of theater apart from occasional school plays. I grew up in the suburbs of New York City, and while we didn't go into the city for cultural events very often, when I was in high school I saw a bit of summer stock on Long Island. And some of the school plays were pretty good—the seniors did a very entertaining production of *My Three Angels* that I still remember.

I would spend a lot of time looking at the theater ads in the Sunday paper, and I always bought *Theatre Arts* magazine, where there were lots of articles and also a new play in every issue—that's where I first encountered Frederick Dürrenmatt's great play *The Visit*, for instance. And you could see a certain amount of theater on television. There was a program on the so-called educational channel in New York called *Play of the Week*, with commercials only during the breaks between acts. I saw some terrific stuff there— for example, a marvelous *Waiting for Godot* with Burgess Meredith and Zero Mostel, which made a lasting impression on me, and was daringly avant-garde by the standards of the day. *The Grass Harp* by Truman Capote was another one they did, and the *Medea* of Euripides with Judith Anderson, and also minor plays, like *The Rope Dancers* by Morton Wishengrad, which I don't think has lived in anybody's memory. At the time I found it very interesting.

And the plays of Eugene O'Neill were a big influence on me when I discovered them as a teenager. My father died almost exactly when I was born, and although my mother remarried when I was three, I was intrigued by the thought of my "real" father—my mother had evidently been pretty traumatized by his death, and she never said a whole lot about him. Some of his old possessions were stuck away in boxes in the basement of our house, and when I was poking around in them one day I ran across a few green volumes from a set of O'Neill's plays. I opened one at random, and while I have no recollection of which play met my eye, I was thunderstruck by the stark emotion and the rawness of language in the words—the polar opposite of the restrained, even repressed daily discourse of my very conservative 1950s household.

Sometime after that I started reading about O'Neill's life, and the amount of awful stuff that went on—the alcohol, the drugs, the suicides, and so on—was also fascinating, worlds away from the kind of proper, rule-following life I'd been taught to regard as normal. Over the years I've seen and/or read all his plays, and I've come to agree with Edmund Wilson's witty aphorism that O'Neill had genius but lacked talent. That said, though, I have tremendous respect for his extraordinary candor and his hugely experimental spirit. Think of it: *The Great God Brown* has all the characters wearing masks, *Strange Interlude* has all the characters speaking their interior monologues aloud, *Mourning Becomes Electra* is a cycle of three full-length dramas, *The Iceman Cometh* and the autobiographical *Long Day's Journey Into Night* are enormously long, and all of these push the limits of what mainstream theater customarily accommodates. The writing may be clunky and the plot may not be subtle—that's where the talent shortage shows—but the conceptual boldness and emotional honesty are where the genius enters in.

Adding one more reminiscence of my own, I did many stints as senior critic at the O'Neill Theater Center in Connecticut, and during one residency there I got to live in the Monte Cristo Cottage, the O'Neill family's summer home. All the furnishings were the same as they'd been during O'Neill's lifetime, and it was wonderful to sit in the cottage, read the description of the set at the beginning of *Long Day's Journey Into Night*, and realize that the true biographical events of the play took place exactly where I was residing. O'Neill still has a real mystique for me.

Every year in high school we had to do a term paper on a writer, and in tenth grade O'Neill was my topic of choice. In eleventh grade I went for my second-favorite playwright, Tennessee Williams, but my English teacher vetoed it—the author of items like *Cat on a Hot Tin Roof* and *Suddenly Last Summer* was too controversial and even scandalous to be acceptable. Or so it seemed to the teacher, but I outfoxed the system. Williams was an extremely well-known cultural figure at the time, and looking in the school's own library, I found enough plays—*The Glass Menagerie*, *A Streetcar Named Desire*, and one or two others—to fulfill the requirement for the paper, so my teacher gave in and allowed me to go ahead.

Then in my senior year I wrote about William Inge, obviously a less important writer but quite interesting to me at the time. Three papers, three playwrights. Unfortunately, few of their plays have been adapted into first-rate movies, although a few of Williams's plays—*Cat on a Hot Tin Roof*, *Suddenly Last Summer*, *The Night of the Iguana*, one or two others—have made it to the screen in reasonably good shape. Poor old O'Neill has suffered some really terrible adaptations.

What did you read as a child and a teenager apart from plays?

Most of it wasn't especially exalted stuff. At the beginning I liked some of the Little Golden Books for very young kids—one about a little girl who goes to the circus with her father has always stayed with me for some reason—and later I was into the Hardy Boys books. After that it was largely science fiction, which a lot of adolescents read, and which I'm still moderately interested in. And comic books, which I loved as a young kid—superhero comics like the Superman, Batman, and Captain Marvel series and comical comics like the Donald Duck and Bugs Bunny lines. I also discovered the Little Lulu comics, which had some of the wittiest and most underappreciated comic-book writing of that time—you read it here first, folks! The old *Mad* comics were brilliant, of course, and *Mad* stayed marvelous when it became a magazine. I was also fascinated by horror comics, although I had to sneak those in because my parents didn't approve. I didn't stay stuck on comics in my teenage years, but later I was happy to learn that some very great filmmakers have been really into comic books, Alain Resnais being one example. Not great literature, but comics kept me reading and made it a steady habit, for which I'm grateful to them.

When did you start seeing more live theater as well as reading plays?

I started going to Broadway shows when I was around high-school age and I still remember things I saw. The first was

My Fair Lady, which was a record-breaking hit in the late 1950s. Next I saw a revue called *La Plume de Ma Tante*, and then *Bye Bye Birdie*, another very big musical at the time. Then I wanted to see a straight play so I saw *The Tenth Man* by Paddy Chayefsky, which is pretty much forgotten today, but I found it really powerful—it's about a bunch of Jewish men and a woman who comes into their midst, and the drama of the story involves what's either a psychiatric crisis or supernatural possession by a dybbuk. Around that time I also saw *The Music Man*, another musical, and in the early 1960s I saw two relatively unconventional plays, Eugène Ionesco's *Rhinoceros*, with Ralph Meeker and Zero Mostel, and Harold Pinter's *The Caretaker*, with Donald Pleasence, Alan Bates, and Robert Shaw. *Rhinoceros* and *The Caretaker* were billed as the first avant-garde plays to hit Broadway, so again I was indulging my early curiosity about works that break the usual molds.

When did you start looking at film in a serious way?

Sometime in late high school I saw a book on a paperback stand, *The Liveliest Art* by Arthur Knight, and had a flash of excitement—wow, it's possible to take movies seriously the way I've been taking theater and literature seriously! And movies are available to me! My town had two movie theaters—one showed single features, one showed double features—and there were other ones I could also get to a lot more easily than going to Manhattan to see a play, which cost a lot of money plus permission from my parents. So I bought the book with great enthusiasm and when I started to read it, I found it dull and dry, full of names and titles and dates. I don't think it was a bad book, but it really bored me at the time, so I decided to stick with theater and reading as my big interests.

But obviously things changed. One of the first times I remember a movie striking me in an artistic way was when I ran across *Citizen Kane* on television. It was an old 1950s-type TV, and the movie was interrupted by commercials, but it was those interruptions that made me realize for the first time that a movie can have a rhythm, the way a piece of music does. I was fairly young at the time, but I was onto something there.

A bigger event happened in my first year at Boston University. A friend suggested going to a movie and said I should choose. I looked in the paper for what was playing nearby, and a sub-run theater, which showed recent films that were past their first runs, was showing a double feature of two French films I had heard of or read something about. The big attraction for me was that you could see both of them for something like a dollar, a real selling point for a couple of college students. They were the first two features by Alain Resnais: *Hiroshima mon amour* and *Last Year at Marienbad*. So we watched them, and my friend was completely bored, but I was riveted, especially by *Last Year at Marienbad*. My friend was totally skeptical and said that if I liked it so much I should explain it to him. It's an extremely puzzling film, of course, and I couldn't begin to explain it, but I had absolutely loved it, and the mystery about it was a big part of its appeal. It was like hearing a new language for the very first time, coming upon some completely new phenomenon that I didn't know existed in the world. I had been to countless movies in my growing up, years but I'd never seen anything like this, and I wanted to be able to understand it. I wanted to have some idea of what was going on here.

So I pursued it and started to go to all the foreign films, the so-called art films, that I could find, exploring this new territory. Boston and Cambridge had a few revival and repertory theaters that showed foreign films and old American films; the most useful were the Fine Arts in Boston and the Brattle across the river. They changed their bills about twice a week, so I could see many foreign films right there in my city. BU had a film society as well, showing 16mm prints of movies from different periods of film history and various places in the world. So I started to give myself a film education.

The movies that showed up most often included Italian neorealist films like Fellini's *La Strada* and *Nights of Cabiria*, great Ingmar Bergman works like *The Seventh Seal* and *Through a Glass Darkly*, and French New Wave pictures like Godard's *Breathless* and Rivette's *Paris Belongs to Us* and Truffaut's *The 400 Blows* and *Jules and Jim*. I also saw Eastern European films like Wajda's *Ashes and Diamonds* and Polanski's *Knife in the Water*. And the Brattle had a recurring Humphrey Bogart festival, timed to Harvard's final-exam schedule. I saw *Casablanca* there with a good friend, and for years thereafter she and I made a point of seeing that splendid picture every time it reappeared. In addition to the movie's excellence, the audience that night was quite a spectacle—everyone knew the film from first scene to last, and they responded to favorite moments with great enthusiasm. When Claude Rains says, "Major Strasser has been shot," booing and hissing broke out all over, and at the same time people were shushing the booers so everyone could hear Rains say, "Round up the usual suspects," whereupon a pandemonium of cheering broke out. I'm a total stickler for quiet in the audience, but that was one occasion when the noise added a delightful dimension to the show.

All this time my college major was English language and literature, but I seriously considered switching from the liberal-arts college to either the film school or the theater school. I didn't make the change because I was afraid that if I did go into film or theater, and it turned out I couldn't make it as an actor or director or some such, then I'd be stuck without any way of making a living. Also, the film school was mostly about production, and I was less inter- ested in making films than in seeing and understanding and thinking about them. So there I was, concerned that majoring in film or theater might leave me unable to make a living. So I stuck with English, where there are hardly any career opportunities—it was what you studied when you didn't know what you wanted to do later in life. But I was actively giving myself a film education, watching movies and also reading about cinema.

There were very few film books in those days, so you couldn't read a lot of extended treatments of the art of cinema, but there were some books and there were certainly articles in magazines and newspapers. Although I didn't read things in a very methodical way, I tried to familiarize myself with what people in the field were saying. I read Pauline Kael's big article "Zeitgeist and Poltergeist; or, Are Movies Going to Pieces?" when it came out in *The Atlantic*, and I thought it was a terrible essay. Years later I knew Pauline and I liked her and respected her in a lot of ways, but to me in 1964 she seemed cantankerous and off base, with tastes and attitudes very different from mine. So that was an early experience with the art of film criticism. In the meanwhile I was going to the movies as often as I could. Everybody else thought I was wasting my life, but I thought I was doing something worthwhile, and it turned out I actually made something of it.

Did you have preferences between American and foreign films when you started to be serious about movies?

I was immediately aware of the traps a lot of intellectuals were falling into—only liking the foreign films, or only liking the silent movies, or some such. I didn't want to be that kind of snob, and I wasn't going to turn my back on all the Hollywood movies that had given me pleasure over the years, so I tried to keep my mind as open as possible.

I was also looking at what certain critics were writing—the ten-best lists of the smarter reviewers, for instance—and I saw that the good critics liked both foreign and domestic movies, which I thought was the right approach.

It's also relevant that rock 'n' roll was another of my great enthusiasms as I was growing up, and I knew that plenty of people—such as my father, who had been a musician for a while—regarded that music as noisy junk and thought the only *real* music was classical music. I thought classical music was just fine, but I was not going to abandon the music I loved most, which was rock'n'roll, by which I mean the doo-wop music of the 1950s and the psychedelic and British Invasion music of the 1960s. I understood that there was great value in popular art as well as so-called high art, and that went for the movies as well.

When you went to college there presumably wasn't an option for studying film, but did you try to incorporate film into your English studies? Or was it mostly extracurricular?

You could get into film production at Boston University, but there was no such thing as film studies, and programs like that were extremely rare in general. I was an English major and in those days what English majors did was study English, which meant words, not motion pictures. I put my movie interests into play once in a while, though. I got an extremely high grade on a paper I wrote about Melville's superb *Bartleby the Scrivener*, where I compared its pace to that of a Resnais movie.

JOURNALISM

When did you first get involved in writing about movies?

That was at college. The *BU News* was the largest-circula-tion college weekly in America, and in my senior year the editor was my close friend Ray Mungo, who later became a widely noted author, and with whom I stayed in touch for years to come. He liked movies, and he knew I was heavily into them, so he promptly made me the film critic. The paper had limited space, so I didn't write that many reviews, but I think the ones I wrote were pretty good—a friend told me my review of the Scandinavian softcore picture *I, a Woman* was the funniest thing he'd seen in the paper. I also had my first experiences of having things shortened, cut, trimmed, and otherwise truncated, sometimes without any input from me, simply because there wasn't room on the page for the whole article. The dark side of journalism! But I didn't expect to keep writing about movies or the arts over the long term. I still didn't know what I was going to do with my life.

Were you still going to the theater at this time?

I was still very interested in theater and I would see plays from time to time. Boston had Broadway shows and pre-Broadway tryouts. I really liked Tennessee Williams— I saw his play *The Milk Train Doesn't Stop Here Anymore* in 1962—and I paid a little attention to local theater groups and college productions. I didn't go to the theater very much, though, now that I was putting a lot of my time into movies. I also listened to music and did a lot of reading, and I had studies to attend to, although I was pretty lackadai-sical in the latter department.

When did you graduate from college, and how did you tran-sition into your first employment?

I entered Boston University in the class of 1966, but in the '60s it was sort of in your contract that you would drop out of college at some point and be a wastrel for a while. I did just that. I must say I had a very protracted adolescence—it went on and on and on. I ended up graduating just a year late, in 1967, and still had no idea what I was going to do. I had taken a couple of education courses at BU, thinking I would probably end up an English teacher or something like that, but that was certainly not my ambition.

Because I had dropped out for a while, I had two or three courses still to do and I had finally run out of money after four years-plus of going to a pretty expensive university. So I needed to get some sort of job. My lingering adolescence was finally starting to end as I went into my twenties, but I didn't have much work experience. Looking at job listings in the papers, I discovered a very small number of options I'd be willing to take on. Then I had a bright idea.

My parents were Christian Scientists, and while I was never fond of the family religion, I was now living in Boston and the central headquarters of the Christian Science Church was right down the street. The church owns and operates *The Christian Science Monitor*, which my parents always had in the house. I was familiar with it. So I thought maybe I should go there and try to get a job. They'll probably ask me if I'm a Christian Scientist, and since my parents had me sign up as a member of the church when I was twelve, I could say "yes" and they could look in their records and see it was true. So I walked down the street, went into the *Monitor* employment office, and asked for a job.

And I got one. It was a real entry-level job, but fine for my purposes: it was indoors, didn't involve selling or lifting, and had to do with words. The position was officially called copy clerk, but informally we were always called copy kids. It was basically being an errand person — you would carry messages from one department to another, fill gluepots, bring people reams of typing paper, and that sort of thing. This was back in the days before automated typesetting. Everyone wrote on typewriters and their copy was set into print on Linotype machines; it was an old-fashioned traditional newspaper operation. And my job had a few advantages. There were adjustable starting times, so you could begin early in the morning and be done early in the afternoon, or start later and be finished later. That appealed to me because I was still not a very disciplined person. Another great advantage was that you could leave the building anytime you wanted and people would assume you were doing an errand. But more important, you got to meet the writers and editors. I met the film critic, for instance. It was just a job for him, like being a reporter with a particular beat, but he was a nice guy.

A big turning point came when I was doing one of the other jobs we copy kids did, which was sitting in for a department clerk who was away on vacation or out sick. At one point the editorial assistant for Arts and Entertainment was away, so somebody had to sit at her desk, answer the phone, and sort the mail. I volunteered, and this let me get better acquainted with the people in the department. I should mention that I never thought I would last on the paper more than a few months while I finished my last courses at school. I thought it was hilarious that a non-religious person like me would be working at that paper. But there I was, and it was a pleasant environment. I also quickly found that the religion, and the church that owned the newspaper, almost never came up. Most of the people there were church members and practicing Christian Scientists, but in the newsroom they were professionals doing their jobs, so I didn't feel ill at ease, and I was rather enjoying the place.

Then one day when I was filling in at the editorial assistant's desk, the arts editor and one of the critics were talking about a local college production they were planning to review. The critic couldn't do it because of a schedule conflict, so he was about to call and cancel the press tickets. Then the art critic, Christopher Andreae, whom I knew very casually, pointed to me and said, "He likes going to plays. Why don't you ask him?" And at that moment I spoke up and I said, "I've reviewed movies for my college paper, and I'd like to give it a try." I'm sure the editor would have been perfectly happy to ignore me, but he said, "All right, and we won't print what you write if we don't like it." I thought that was fair!

So I went off to this production by the Harvard Dramatic Club. If I remember correctly, it was Christopher Fry's play *The Lady's Not for Burning*, and it wasn't very well done, so I started my professional writing career with a negative review. The editor sat down and went over it with me and made a few changes, taking out a slightly technical term and so forth. But it went straight into print. As planned, it ran in the New England edition of the *Monitor*—the paper published five editions a day at that time—and they put my name on it and I was very pleased. I mailed a copy to my parents and they were pleased as well. Maybe they thought I was finally getting religion.

Criticism

Did you have a clear concept of film criticism at this time?

I'd been reading movie criticism, mostly in the form of newspaper and magazine reviews, though not in a very organized or systematic way. And I had a fairly humble attitude when I started writing professionally. When I started to think I might be able to make some sort of a career or at least a steady gig out of this, my idea was to do it correctly, not to be experimental or blaze new trails. That might come later, but for the time being, I wanted to write good articles that would get printed and would let me get a foot in the door of this line of work.

This suggests that you weren't yet thinking about having a particular writing style.

I was very aware of being a beginner, and I knew I was writing for a general-audience newspaper, although the *Monitor* thought of itself as having reasonably thoughtful readers. There was a certain way in which general-audience newspaper reviews were written, and I wanted to master that craft. Finding my own voice or coming up with my own sense of style would come in time. For now it was a question of writing in the correct manner for that kind of newspaper in that time and that place. This said, however, my opinions were my opinions, so even though I wasn't trying to come up with new ways of writing reviews or articles, I was certainly interested in expressing my opinions, my point of view, my perspective on things. That's what would make my reviews distinctive, assuming I succeeded at what I was trying to do.

How did things develop after your first article was published?

Other opportunities came along, one by one at first, and then pretty quickly when editors saw I could handle things. My next article was again suggested by Chris Andreae. A gallery in Boston was showing work by a group of San Francisco artists who cultivated a whimsical style called Funk Art, and along with this the gallery was showing some non-narrative experimental films. Chris was going to review the show and asked me to review the films; he shared the now-antiquated idea that if it moves it isn't really art, and movies do indeed move. I already had some exposure to avant-garde cinema, so I was happy to take this on.

Then over the next few weeks and months I became an all-purpose reviewer. There was a reasonably small staff at the *Monitor*, and things would come along that the regular critics didn't have time for or care about. I wrote about the movies and theater productions that none of the others wanted to bother with, usually for the New England edition of the paper but sometimes for the all-editions page. I was able to build up a portfolio of articles, all during my very early months of working there, when I was still doing clerk jobs and doing the writing on the side. There was a theater critic and a music critic in Boston and a couple of film critics in New York, and there was also a young all-purpose critic, which is what I was becoming. I would get the assignments none of the others wanted, and that was fine with me. I was a newcomer, I had no particular training, I had never been to journalism school, but I was building up a body of work. And I was getting paid for each piece, which was nice, since we clerks didn't make a whole lot of money. I wrote about movies that are now forgotten even by me. I reviewed the Moscow circus. I was even given my own column to write. In the late '60s it was becoming fashionable for publications to take pop music seriously, a sign of the growing power of youth culture in that era, and the *Monitor* decided to get in on the trend. They called my column The Pop Scene, which is hardly original or clever, but it allowed me to keep following the music I loved and provided me with a steady flow of free rock albums. Another welcome perk. And along the way I got to know many interesting *Monitor* writers and editors, including the editor-in-chief, Erwin D. Canham, who was then a legendary figure in American journalism.

I also wrote about little theater companies that were working in Boston at the time, the kind of stuff that was done in church basements and meeting halls and places like that. And I found that in some of these cases the people were making up for their lack of means by using real imagination. For one example, I remember seeing a production of a minor play by Bertolt Brecht, the *Baden Lehrstück*, by some little group; they just had a couple of props and a coat rack, and they used them in all kinds of inventive ways, and they used their bodies in all kinds of inventive ways. Decades later I still remember that, not vividly but fondly, and that sort of show was worthwhile for me as a spectator as well as a fledgling journalist. And of course I was still going to see things on my own. When the Living Theatre passed through town, for instance, I saw all four of the productions they did at the MIT theater. Truly memorable events.

How did you become an official Monitor *staff writer?*

Somebody retired and there was a reshuffling of the Arts and Entertainment department, making room for another person on the full-time staff. I had been clerking for a about a year when I became a staff writer. Instead of doing my writing on the side it was now the main part of my work, and all the writers in the Boston office also did editorial tasks—editing other people's articles, laying out the page, writing the headlines and cutlines, as photo captions were called. At first I was the fourth-string critic to everybody else. This meant I didn't do much writing about the major films or the big theater and music productions, but looking at the more marginal items meant seeing a good deal of youthful and experimental work, some of which was very good. And I still wrote about a variety of things, mainly movies and theater and music. I made a point of writing about anything I could, no matter how minor, and sometimes a fairly major thing would be available to me.

I was still in the throes of excitement about auteur theory, and many admirable critics worshipped Howard Hawks as one of the great screen artists. His 1970 swan song *Rio Lobo* got to Boston before the New York critics had reviewed it; for them it was just another western, but for me it was a chance to expound on Hawks's directorial greatness. I was sick at the time, with a very bad cold, and the weather was rotten. But that wasn't going to stop me. I bundled up in warm clothes, got my wife to hold me up on my way to the theater, saw the thing, and wrote my review. I don't remember what I wrote, but I was delighted to go on record about what turned out to be Hawks's last picture. I also enjoyed a trip to an avant-garde film festival in Maine. The third-string film critic with a little seniority over me had agreed to cover the festival, only to realize that he had absolutely no knowledge or ideas about experimental cinema, so he asked me to go along. The films we saw included *Chinese Firedrill*, a good but now-forgotten film by Will Hindle, and *Relativity* by the gifted filmmaker and science-fiction illustrator Ed Emshwiller, whom I later got to know and liked very much.

And all along I continued my autodidactic education in cinema. This was in the years before video, remember, so you had to somehow get yourself to where a film was being shown, and that was especially tricky with avant-garde and noncommercial films. It was easier to see a certain amount of unconventional or unorthodox theater, because of groups that were experimenting along those lines in and around Boston, so I probably saw more experimental theater than experimental film back then. And some of it was excellent. The Harvard Dramatic Club did some good work, as did the Agassiz Theatre Company, another Cambridge troupe, founded by Timothy Mayer and Thomas Babe, tremendously inventive talents. I can't remember many of the plays they put on way back then, but I do recall seeing a production of *Peace* by Aristophanes, directed by Mayer and starring Susan Channing, who later changed her first name to Stockard and became a successful movie actress. There was also a production based on the Book of Job, with God's voice coming from a whirlwind represented by one of those hand-spun merry-go-rounds you find in playgrounds. Very clever and highly effective.

Boston After Dark

How long did you continue at the Monitor *with that arrangement?*

As mentioned earlier, I started at the *Monitor* in early 1967 and became a staff writer in 1968. Then in 1969 I left the paper for a while. I was offered the position of editor of an alternative weekly called *Boston After Dark*, and I liked the idea of getting away from the *Monitor*, which was owned and operated by a church I wasn't interested in and was fairly conservative in its tastes and approach to culture. When I became a staff writer, the editor of the paper had congratulated me and added a comment I still remember: "The *Monitor* does not support the general moral decline." That was a silly statement, of course—what does it even mean? I had a reasonable amount of freedom in what I could write and the paper would publish, but the idea of running a weekly paper with a young readership was very refreshing.

So there I went, and there I stayed for many months. *BAD* was an interesting paper. During my time as editor we doubled its size, reaching a very large readership among young people in and around Boston. The publishers were also starting similar papers in other cities—*Philadelphia After Dark*, *Cleveland After Dark*—and the enterprise was thriving in many ways. But there were big problems, most notably that we were understaffed and there weren't enough people to handle things like doubling the size of the paper. So after a while I stepped down as editor and gave myself a new position I created: senior critic. I wrote a regular column called Captain Everything, which allowed me to comment on different kinds of art and culture in the freewheeling environment that *BAD* provided.

But problems persisted, and it started to appear that one of the publishers was taking dubious liberties with the paper's tax filings. All kinds of chaos ensued and the paper collapsed. The collapse was sudden but also intricate, involving a staff walkout, which included me, and a rival paper. One of the publishers tried to keep the operation going under another name—*Publick Occurrences*, hardly a catchy moniker—and after a complicated series of events the *BAD* publisher bought up its main rival, the *Cambridge*

Phoenix, and used the name *Boston Phoenix* for the new incarnation. But by then I was gone.

What did you do?

I scurried back to the establishment press as quickly as my legs would carry me. I did some freelance writing for the *Boston Herald-Traveler*, which offered to hire me at one point, but mainly, I got myself back to the *Monitor* and they were glad to have me.

Did you continue the same kinds of work when you returned?

Yes. I returned to the monitor in 1970, if memory serves, and went into several years of being very content. I was free to write about many different things in many different art forms, and I began to develop certain subspecialties. The paper's theater critics in New York and Boston had absolutely no interest in experimental or avant-garde work, which interested me a great deal, so I had all of that material to myself.

Similarly, the music critic had very little interest in experimental or avant-garde music, including the minimalism of Philip Glass and Steve Reich, which fascinated me, so that also became a specialty of mine, along with electronic music and other unconventional developments in musical culture. I also got involved with dance. I have fond memories of an early interview with Pilobolus, the dance company started by four Dartmouth grads whose involvement in athletics led them to take a course in dance that thrilled them so much they decided to make dancing their life's work. Three of them came to Boston for our interview—Jonathan Wolken, Robby Barnett, and Rob Pendleton, later known as Moses Pendleton—and a few hours after we talked, Rob phoned me at home to say they couldn't get the train back to New Hampshire for some reason I don't remember, maybe a snowstorm. So I invited them to my apartment, where they slept on the floor, and Jonathan entertained my kids with his banjo. Soon afterward I spent some time in their New Hampshire digs, gathering material to flesh out the long feature article I wrote about them. In subsequent years they became a major presence in modern dance.

So I did all kinds of critical writing. At one point I compared the nature of my job to a big overstuffed chair that you've been sitting in for years and years, so its contours have shaped to your body and it fits you just right, although it wouldn't fit anybody else. Also, by this time I was married and had a couple of very young kids, so covering events in and around Boston suited me well. I did some traveling, of course—for example, going to a national college theater festival in Baltimore, where I saw some marvelous work by energetic, inventive young people—but surveying the Boston scene was my main work, and I was happy with it.

By the way, I should mention some big music festivals of the late '60s. I'd been to the Newport Folk Festival as a civilian, so to speak, and while we had a good time, it would have been a lot better if the cheap seats weren't a million miles from the stage. Going again as an accredited journalist, not only did I have excellent seats, but the press had its own refreshment stand so we didn't have to elbow our way through the crowds. Very nice.

And yes, I went to Woodstock, the legendary festival of 1969. My wife and I drove there with a couple of close friends and pitched a tent on the grounds of what appeared to be some sort of old-folks home, which was excellent, since they cheerfully let us use their bathrooms. Everyone we encountered was kind and generous despite the fact that literally hundreds of thousands of scruffy youngsters were invading their town and swarming all over the place. As for the music, I didn't like the idea of concerts lasting for hours and hours and hours, so I found a nice little bar where I could observe the festivities from afar. It worked out splendidly.

On another topic, I know you're very interested in politics. Were you always comfortable with the Monitor's *editorial positions on public and political matters?*

Good question. Generally speaking, the paper was way more conservative than I was, but they didn't usually push their political views too hard, partly because the paper was owned and operated by a church that didn't want to alienate its members, although the members tended to be pretty conservative as well. But on some important matters the paper and I were basically in sync. They opposed capital punishment, as I did. And even though Christian Scientists eschew medical treatment for themselves, the paper believed in freedom of choice—as a minority religion with eccentric practices, they didn't want government to intervene in this area—and that extended to a pro-choice position on abortion, which I also shared. So in arenas like these I was happier at the *Monitor* than I would have been at, say, one of the right-wing tabloids.

THEATER, MUSIC
AND NEW YORK

When did you move to New York?

Sometime in 1974 an arts writer retired or resigned and the department was reshuffled again. Two of the critics in New York had been sharing the film reviews, with me as a backup in the Boston office, and then the field was narrowed to the New York critic, Louise Sweeney, and me. Louise was a nice person and a capable writer, but there had been some conflicts over turf when I wrote about something she wanted to review. In any case, the movies of the '70s were getting too sexy and violent for her, so she asked for a transfer to the Washington bureau, where she did interviews with people in the news. The editors sensibly decided it would be better to have a single film critic, and I grabbed the job as soon as they offered it. New York was the national hub of film criticism, and I was from the New York suburbs, so I was happy to return. We bought a house on Long Island, not too far from where I grew up. I had a desk at the paper's New York Bureau, and I put in appearances there from time to time, but I did most of my writing at home, which I'd been doing ever since I became a staff writer.

On a side note, as the '70s progressed I realized it was a great time to be a journalist. The coverage of Watergate by *The Washington Post* and *The New York Times* made a lot of people regard reporters as cultural and political heroes, and a little of that prestige spilled over to newspaper work in general. It's also worth mentioning that when the Pentagon Papers were published, exposing all sorts of information about the Vietnam War that had been withheld until that time, the *Monitor* was one of the newspapers that printed some of the material as the government fought court battles trying to keep the disclosures under wraps. Spielberg's movie *The Post* deals with all this, and I was pleased to see the *Monitor* flash across the screen at one point. The situation is very different nowadays, with much of the gullible public falling for bogus accusations of "fake news" and so forth, but once upon a time it felt good to call yourself a journalist.

How did relocating to New York change your activities?

Right after moving, it hit me how much more culture was available to me. New York is the cultural capital of the United States, and in some ways of the world. I now had the whole movie field to myself, but there was also Broadway and Off-Broadway theatre, great concert halls, and so on. So I made the very dubious decision to steer away from the smaller-scale experimental and avant-garde work and devote my attention to the big-time material, like Broadway productions and other major events.

Then came an eye-opening experience. Some of the New York avant-garde theater groups had teamed up on a little festival of their work, either new works or pieces that were still in progress. It was basically a way to get some extra publicity, but I thought it would be fun to touch bases with that scene again, so I decided to choose a few events and write an article.

One of the productions was by the Performance Group, and I had once traveled from Boston to New York to see their adaptation of the *Bacchae* of Euripides, called *Dionysus in '69*. It was directed by Richard Schechner, the founder and proprietor of the Performance Group, and I'd been extremely impressed by it. Now they were doing Seneca's *Oedipus*, so I promptly put that on my schedule. Then I saw that the group was doing another show, called *Rumstick Road*, on the same night in the same theater—the Performing Garage in Soho—and you could see this if you stayed a little later and went to the smaller performance space upstairs, which I decided to do. *Oedipus* was a very solid production, as I'd expected, and then I went upstairs for the 10 o'clock show of the other piece. When I looked at the program I saw that this was the follow-up to an earlier piece I hadn't seen, so I thought about leaving and heading for home. But there I was, so I stayed and watched it. And it was an important night for me.

Rumstick Road was directed by Richard's assistant, Elizabeth LeCompte, who was working with a few members of the Performance Group and some others she had recruited. The star and main character of the show was her partner, Spalding Gray, who became a legendary figure and a good friend. It was performed by four people in a large room with one modestly constructed set and the audience sitting on bleachers. And it absolutely floored me. The visual imagination and theatrical inventiveness on display in the next hour and a quarter were staggering, all accomplished with a few props, a slide projector showing images from Spalding's early life, and tape recordings of family members talking about his mother's suicide, which was a main subject of the piece. I'll give one example of the brilliance and inventiveness of the show. At one point Spalding reads a letter he received from his mother during one of her breakdowns, and a slide of her face is projected onto Spalding's face, so the two of them become a single image, and as he reads his voice becomes increasingly frantic, echoing the manic tone of the letter itself, and the concluding "Love, Mom" turns

into a hysterical shriek. The moment is thrilling in its inge-
nuity and chilling in its effect.

Some aspects of *Rumstick Road* felt especially close to
me on a personal level, since like me, Spalding had been raised
as a Christian Scientist, and that was a prominent element in
the show. So I saw it again to make sure that my personal
experience wasn't leading me to overpraise the production,
but no, it was every bit as amazing as I'd thought. Seeing
it was a revelation, and I immediately wanted to get better
acquainted with these people. I already knew Liz LeCompte
a bit, but I met Spalding, did some interviews with him, and
saw the play a number of times.

One big result of all this was that I abandoned my very
temporary resolution to pay more attention to large-scale
events and less attention to smaller-scale ones. This was a
small-scale work, and one of the most brilliant things I had
ever seen. Later the group revived the earlier show, *Sakonnet
Point*, so I was able to catch up with it, and eventually their
first three pieces based on Spalding's life and memories —
Sakonnet Point, *Rumstick Road*, and the equally superb
Nayatt School — were designated as a trilogy, *Three Places
in Rhode Island*. These were followed by the epilogue *Point
Judith* and the concluding *Route 1&9: The Last Act*, and then
many other works not rooted in Spalding's experiences. After
he died — he committed suicide, as his mother had done — the
group ranged into different territories with varying degrees
of success. The Wooster Group is still very much around, and
I keep up with their work as best I can.

I'll briefly add that Spalding and Liz set up a theater
workshop for kids in the '70s, and my twins were in it
for a couple of years when they were about six or seven,
running around the Performing Garage and giving ideas to
the grownups. Liz's style calls for relatively chaotic content
framed in a visually rigorous manner, and watching little
kids cut loose and improvise was surely a source of inspiration.

*Were there any other memorable performances you saw
during that time?*

Of course, although none of them topped the early productions by the Wooster Group, as Liz's group came to be called.
Another memorable experience was seeing the legendary
Einstein on the Beach by Robert Wilson and Philip Glass at
the Metropolitan Opera House, in its first American performance after touring through various European countries.
This was my first exposure to minimalist music, and also to

the radical kind of avant-garde theater that Wilson was still developing around that time. I can't say I was overwhelmingly impressed by it, I was more bemused and intrigued by it. Here was a show about four-and-a-half hours long, with no intermission, no linear plot, performed in extreme slow motion, with a stage setting that was mostly grays, on which Wilson painted with his lights. It was a new experience, for me and for everyone. It was quite the spectacle, but it took me a while to think about it and come to terms with it.

A slightly shortened version of the music—or what you might call the soundtrack, since there's a fair amount of speaking as well—was released on the Tomato Records label, and I listened to it constantly. Then I met an assistant editor at *Rolling Stone* who suggested that I interview Bob Wilson, and I agreed, since I wanted to hear his version of what he was trying to accomplish. So I went to his loft on Vestry Street and spoke with him for quite a while. At first his manner was positively robotic, as if absolute self-control was part of his image. But by the end of the interview he had really loosened up, and I felt we had established a good rapport. He was concerned about how he could manage to keep working in his own radical style in American venues, given the commercialism and conservatism of American theater. I suggested doing shows in museums or galleries and he insisted he didn't *want* museums or galleries, he wanted major stages in major theaters. He was determined to work on a grand scale.

I asked him how he first came upon his aesthetic, and he said he didn't really know, but when he was a kid he would sometimes come downstairs in the night and rearrange all the glasses in the kitchen cabinet! So that urge to arrange things, to organize things, to put things into his own configurations obviously went back to the early stages of his life. I spoke with Wilson a few other times over the years and always found him forthcoming and pleasant. And he completely succeeded in his goal of reaching vast audiences without compromising his style in the least. The newsletters from his organization, the Byrd Hoffman Water Mill Foundation, named after a mentor who helped him get over a childhood stutter, shows that he is all over the planet, putting on plays, operas, and his own theater pieces here, there, and everywhere. He's a major force in modern theater.

Minimalism

My experience with Philip Glass has been similar. After my first contact via *Einstein on the Beach*, I interviewed and talked with him a number of times in many different places. I once took a taxi with him to a rehearsal and held in my hands the original handwritten score of *Einstein on the Beach*. He was always forthcoming and enjoyable to talk with, and I went to every recital and concert of his that I could get to, following his music very closely for many years. His music director, Michael Riesman, became a good personal friend. In a nice coincidence, Michael's wife, Mayra Langdon Riesman, did film publicity and also founded the online publication *Film Scouts*, which I wrote for on occasion.

And then there's the other great minimalist composer, Steve Reich, who was also rising in the ranks during the 1970s. I got to know Steve and interviewed him a few times. At one point he recruited me to speak on a panel about minimalism and the arts at Virginia Commonwealth University, where we went on a private plane owned by one of Steve's patrons. He was always very articulate about his work and a real pleasure to talk with. His music was often quite abstract in its early period—*Four Organs, Drumming, Six Pianos, Music for 18 Musicians*—but he was also very political, which shows clearly in pieces like *Come Out* and *The Desert Music*, and he often taps directly into his Jewish identity, as in *Tehillim* and *Different Trains*. He seemed quite pleased when I said my parents had taught me the old notion that you shouldn't talk to strangers about politics or religion, whereas that's what he does in some of his finest pieces! A work like *The Desert Music* is profoundly political in its outcry against nuclear weapons—at one point a cello intrudes with a glissando that sounds like an air-raid siren—and a work like *Tehillim*, one of his most brilliant ever, is deeply religious. He has also worked with his wife, the video artist Beryl Korot, on projects with a strong religious dimension.

In the '70s it was fashionable for certain artists to work in multiple formats, and none did that more than Meredith Monk, a composer, singer, pianist, choreographer, and occasional filmmaker. I liked much of her work, and after an interview she asked me to do the liner notes for one of her albums, *Our Lady of Late*. I was also fond of her occasional collaborator Ping Chong, who did some splendid work on the Off-Off-Broadway scene. But as much as I liked and admired these artists, I didn't always come up with enthusiastic reviews of particular works. For years I attended every event in the Brooklyn Academy of Music's annual Next Wave Festival, and the 1984 edition opened with *The Games*, a music-theater piece by Meredith and Ping that I found distinctly underwhelming. Most of the other reviewers gushed about it, so I was a lonely skeptical voice. One of the BAM publicists told me that even the people in her office were surprised by all the raves, so I didn't think I was altogether off base.

I also followed Richard Foreman and his marvelously named Ontological-Hysteric Theater, and the Mabou Mines troupe, where Philip Glass had done much of his early work and where JoAnne Akalaitis was very active. I got to know so many tremendously interesting people! And my involvement with cutting-edge music and theater led to a growing interest in dance, as well. I saw and sometimes reviewed classical ballet—the American Ballet Theater, the New York City Ballet, visiting troupes when they came to town—and did the same with modern dance, watching performances and interviewing terrific choreographers like Twyla Tharp, Merce Cunningham, Lucinda Childs, and Pina Bausch.

You were seeing all these musical and theater works and talking with all these people while also being the Monitor *film critic? You must have been busy.*

I was. But I always said I'd rather give my attention to a first-rate theater piece or a first-rate piece of music than to a third- or fourth-rate movie.

I don't share your affection for minimalist music.

You're not alone. Many people don't.

Can you explain why that music has such strong appeal for you?

More than one factor is in play. For whatever reason, I respond strongly to certain kinds of repetition. I like it in poetry, from old English ballads to modern villanelles, and in prose works, like some of Gordon Lish's terrific fiction. Also in Islamic art that uses geometric repetition to comply with the Muslim prohibition of figurative images. It can also be enormously expressive in dance—when Paul Taylor's dancers swirl in circles with outstretched arms in *Arden Court* and *Aureole*, for instance. One of the most powerful dance performances I ever saw was a piece by Laura Dean simply called *Dance*, with a mesmerically repetitive score and a motif of pure circularity that had me riveted throughout. One way of putting this is to compare minimalist music with music in the older Western classical tradition. In traditional music, especially from the classical and romantic periods, the melody line is like a narrative line, always moving and shifting and taking you from one development to the next. In minimalist music the pace may be fast or slow but the development is always slow. Instead of a narrative to follow, it's like an environment to inhabit. And part of the appeal is very simple—when you hear something that's nice and interesting and pleasing, why not hear it a few more times before going on to the next thing?

And to look at this from one more angle, some of the purest minimalist music, such as Glass and Wilson's *Einstein on the Beach*, and Glass's *Music in 12 Parts*, and Reich's *Music for 18 Musicians*, and early works by John Adams, et cetera, taps into the great love of classic rock'n'roll that I had as a kid and still retain to some degree. Classic rock, from the 1950s and early '60s, is thoroughly minimalistic—steady beat, no dissonance, limited chord progressions, not at all unlike minimalist works from the classical-music tradition. When I was a guest on *New, Old and Unexpected*, the innovative show that my friend Tim Page had on WNYC years ago, I did something I thought was a bit mischievous, playing *I Put a Spell on You* by Screamin' Jay Hawkins, which is radical minimalism avant la lettre. I also paired a Meredith Monk vocal with *She Say (Oom Dooby Doom)* by the Diamonds, a song with a swooping high-register vocal, and I played a few other items that showed how minimalist composition was foreshadowed in '50s pop. Of course '50s rock is more primitive, but that's one of its fascinations—it's basically a matter of three chords and three minutes, now show what you can do! Creating vibrant work within strict parameters is a marvelous challenge, in pop music, minimalist music, poetic forms like the sonnet and the villanelle, and even the classic TV sitcom. Et cetera!

Kids

You've mentioned your children a few times. Did you take them to movies and performances you reviewed? What was that like?

Jeremy and Craig were born in 1971 and are identical twins. I wanted to give them a good cultural education, and my work was well suited to that. When they were very young I took them—either both of them or just one of them—to a lot of movies, most of them worthwhile or at least not worthless. We often went to movie theaters, and sometimes I'd bring them along to a critics' screening, and occasionally to an interview I'd set up. One occasion I remember was seeing Peter Weir's *Gallipoli* with them at the Paramount screening room in the Gulf & Western Building, just the three of us at a screening set up for me so I could go directly to an interview with Peter someplace nearby. The finale of that movie shows a character being shot down, and I heard both kids gasp when it happened—it was a sort of stereo gasp, since I was sitting between them, and I could tell they'd really been absorbed in the film. They also went to a great many theater and music events with me. Examples are too numerous to list, but I took them to countless dance and theater events in the annual Next Wave Festival at the Brooklyn Academy of Music, and it was fun seeing Peter Sellars's productions of Mozart's three Da Ponte operas in the late '80s with one or both of them. I enjoyed introducing them to Philip Glass when *Satyagraha* premiered at Artpark in upstate New York, and they got to know the Wooster Group gang very well.

These experiences evidently stuck with them. Neither of them became artists or performers, but both of them have been close to culture ever since. For high school they were accepted into the very competitive LaGuardia School of Music and the Arts, right next door to Lincoln Center, where Craig was in the art division and Jeremy was in the music division with his violin. Jeremy and Tanya Van Sant, his girlfriend and now wife, then started ArtBase, a hugely successful software service for art galleries, museums, and collectors, which kept them in close contact with art and artists, some of them at the pinnacle of the field. Craig went in a different direction, first as an AIDS counselor, than as a medical writer and editor, now as the chief of an environmental consultancy, and he's still my frequent companion for days and nights at the opera. Jeremy and Tanya now divide their time between lower Manhattan and upstate New York, and Craig lives in Vermont with his partner, Kim Souza, who runs her own business and participates in local politics. I'm happy to report that we talk about movies and music to this day.

Traveling

Returning to the nature of your work as a critic, was much traveling involved?

Yes, and that brings up an interesting issue. Back in the 1970s the *Monitor*, like many other papers, allowed writers to go on junkets paid for by interested parties to get material for articles. This included the film critic, and my predecessor had done this for years. So I inherited the ability to do it, and I made any number of trips to Los Angeles and other parts of the world to visit movie sets, talk with movie people, and gather material. I remember going to London when a *Pink Panther* movie was in production—that's where I met Blake Edwards and Peter Sellers, and saw Sellers disrupt shot after shot after shot by breaking into laughter while the camera was rolling—and I watched the volatile Dan Curtis repeatedly lose his temper while shooting *Burnt Offerings* with Bette Davis, Oliver Reed, et al. I also flew to the Netherlands to interview Richard Attenborough and the fine actor Hardy Kruger about *A Bridge Too Far*. Attenborough talked about the daunting logistics of filming an epic World War II picture, where the huge amounts of personnel and equipment made it hard to concentrate on all the fine details. When the movie was finished I didn't give it a very positive review—attention to fine details was exactly what it needed and didn't have. And since the *Monitor* was a family newspaper, I went to Greece with a few other journalists to talk with people involved in the new *Benji* movie. Et cetera. And not all of my excursions were related to movies. I went to Nashville to write about Opryland, the Grand Ole Opry's theme park, where I talked with Dolly Parton and other country-music notables. And there were times I could take the family along. I made a couple of trips to Florida, where the Ringling Bros. and Barnum & Bailey Circus had its winter quarters, and I have a photo of myself and my five-year-old kids talking with Gunther Gebel-Williams, the celebrated animal trainer.

My most unusual junket was a visit to Bermuda for an article about *The Deep*, the scuba-diving adventure movie based on Peter Benchley's novel. It was fun hanging out with the likes of Jacqueline Bisset, but the best part was putting on scuba gear for a tour of the underwater set. Back home I did more scuba diving, even getting advanced certification in the sport. Those days are long behind me now.

Then the *Monitor* changed its policy and stopped participating in press junkets, which was definitely the right thing to do. The practice was fairly corrupt, because you were writing about things you wouldn't have written about if somebody weren't giving you this nice trip. So hey, I did it for a while, and the paper finally came to its senses, and that activity came to an end, and I felt a little cleaner as a result. But there was some value in hobnobbing with other journalists on these occasions. Once a movie company flew a bunch of us to a press event with Richard Dreyfuss, who was starring in a new picture called *Inserts*, written and directed by John Byrum, who's largely forgotten today. The protagonist is a formerly important filmmaker who has outlived his talent, and as the tagline puts it, "Now he's making pornos. But they're brilliant pornos." *Inserts* itself was far from brilliant. Pretty much everyone on the junket thought it was terrible, and poor Richard Dreyfuss had to do a press conference the day after the screening. But unlike the movie he was plugging, he was admirable, defending the picture as far as he plausibly could—he'd agreed to star in it because he thought the script was "the best one-act play" he'd ever read—and reacting to the negative vibes with humor and modesty. Almost twenty-five years later I did an onstage interview with Richard as the centerpiece of a career tribute to him at the World Film Festival in Montreal, and again he was engaging, good-natured, and sharp as a tack. I've never ranked him at the top of the acting profession, but off the screen he's likable and smart.

The Thousand Eyes

Did you write for publications other than the Monitor *in the 1970s?*

After an interview I did with George Stevens Jr., who is the son of the great Hollywood director and was the head of the American Film Institute, the editor of the AFI magazine, *American Film*, asked me to write an article about a couple of issues I had discussed with George, evidently to George's pleasure. That was a one-shot, but I was connected for a while with *The Thousand Eyes*, which billed itself as The Magazine of Public Cinema, a rather grand designation. It was published by Sid Geffen and his wife Jackie Raynal, friends of mine who owned and operated the Carnegie Hall Cinema, next to the fabled concert hall, and the Bleecker Street Cinema, in Greenwich Village, both valuable revival-and-repertory theaters. Sid was a moviehouse entrepreneur and Jackie was a filmmaker, and they were a bit of an odd couple, since Sid was sort of dumpy and Jackie was a Frenchwoman with a mildly glamorous air. The magazine grew out of Sid's desire for a program guide that would give schedules and so forth for his theaters but also have articles and information with wide appeal to what we now call cinephiles. I don't remember many details of the enterprise, but I was on the editorial board, and young writers like Jonathan Rosenbaum and Dan Yakir were also in the mix. It was mildly interesting venture, although the publication didn't last very long, and it could be hard getting Sid to pay up promptly for articles.

Earlier you said that when you started at the Monitor *it was a traditional newspaper with Linotype machines and so forth. When was the paper modernized?*

I don't remember exactly, but it must have been in the early 1980s. I had been writing for years on a portable typewriter, using carbon paper for a second copy, and sending my articles by mail or occasionally phoning one in, and all this was fine with me. The big advantage I saw in switching to an electronic system was that typesetting wouldn't involve a worker in the composing room retyping the articles—errors constantly crept in, and the proofreaders let them pass all too often. The first electronic gizmo they gave me was a dedicated word processor made by a company called Teleram, and by later standards it was fairly primitive. Words appeared on the screen as you typed, but the text was ragged until you pressed an "integrate" key, whereupon the lines and sentences snapped into place. You saved the article on a floppy disc that was indeed floppy, and you transmitted material to the Boston office by putting your phone into an acoustic modem. It all worked pretty well. For traveling I used a smaller, portable machine—I can't remember what it was called—with a tiny screen that was very cramped but sufficed for its intended purpose. In the middle '80s the paper set me up with an IBM computer, which was all the rage at the time, and I used it for at least one of my books as well as all my *Monitor* writing. Eventually they gave me a Mac laptop that I could use in my office and when traveling. This was all quite a change from the old days, and I feel privileged to have started my career in an old hot-type setup, spending considerable time in the composing room, looking over the page with a technician when last-minute adjustments and trims were needed. When I was editor of *Boston After Dark* we used a printing shop with a photo-offset system, colloquially known as cold type, but for me the hot-type system was just fine. All these changes were a kind of subplot to my actual writing career.

Video

Did your viewing habits change when movies started coming out on video? Did that affect your work as a critic?

It changed the movie scene enormously. You could see a film that wasn't playing at a nearby theater! Movies had been shown on TV, of course, but now you had more control over the situation. When home video was just starting up, a friend of mine mused that in the future when he got bored, he'd just pick up his *Citizen Kane* cassette and pleasantly while away the time.

It wasn't quite as simple as that, because only a limited number of movies were available, and the quality of the image and sound were pretty low. I resisted watching films on videocassettes unless there was some good reason for it. I wrote a *Monitor* article about this in the '80s, saying that movies are larger than life but TV is smaller than life, and at the time that made sense. But the advent of DVDs improved things, and the advent of flatscreens and Blu-rays improved them more, and streaming video is a terrific medium. It's true that nothing beats a crisp new 35mm print properly projected on a nice big theatrical screen, but in theaters there's always a danger of improper projection, noisy people, and so on.

And whatever people like Christopher Nolan and Quentin Tarantino think, there's no law of nature saying film is invariably better than video. A few years ago my friend Godfrey Cheshire came to the Walters Art Museum, which happens to be down the street from where I live in Baltimore, to host a screening of *Taste of Cherry*, the great Kiarostami picture. The Walters promoted it heavily: Shown on 35mm film! See it the way Kiarostami intended! And what a letdown it proved to be—the print was faded, spliced, and splotchy, and showing a good Blu-ray edition would have been vastly preferable. I also remember a screening I hosted at the Museum of Modern Art to launch my first book on Jean-Luc Godard. I love that museum, and the event drew a very good crowd—that's where I met Jean-Luc's sister, Veronica, who had never seen *Puissance de la parole*, which was also on the program—but MoMA's print of *Weekend* was so faded that all the colors had turned into magenta. Again, a fine video copy would have been better. So I part company with the film-on-film purists.

California

I know you've lived mostly on the East Coast, but you were on the West Coast for a while too.

Yes indeed. I was born and raised on Long Island, then spent about a dozen years in Boston and environs, then moved back to Long Island and thence to lower Manhattan, where I lived for about two decades, mostly at 176 Broadway in an apartment of which I have fond memories. When my girl-friend (who's now my wife, as you know) took a job chairing the Humanities Department at the Pacifica Graduate Insti-tute, we moved to California and got a house in Ojai, a small city near Santa Barbara, where Pacifica is located. We chose Ojai at my suggestion, because in my early *Monitor* days I would copy-edit dispatches from the annual Ojai Music Festival, which was a very interesting, very adventurous event. The flaw in my reasoning about living there was that the music festival is a three-day event, and there are 362 other days in the year! And during those other days we found Ojai to be a rather dull place. The weather was lovely, the streets were clean, the people were pleasant, and we made some fine friends there, but we missed the big-city vibe we were accustomed to. And then Pacifica turned out to be far too New Age-y for comfort. So notorious Baltimore, the city of *The Wire* and urban problems galore, started to seem like very heaven. We scurried back to Baltimore and our old jobs after about two Californian years and have been there ever since. Baltimore isn't my favorite place—Manhattan is where I feel most comfortable—but by comparison with the West Coast it's just marvelous.

INTERVIEWS AND ACQUAINTANCES

Let's get back to Monitor *articles you've written. Who are some of the people you've interviewed?*

I became a full-time film critic in the 1970s, an interesting time for American movies, since—and I'm not the first to say this—some of the grand old Hollywood auteurs were still active even as the cultural upheavals of the '60s were reverberating through American culture. Something for everyone. Most of the memorable people I've met, talked with, and interviewed crossed my path in New York or during my travels, but there were a few important encounters in Boston as well.

The most illustrious person I met there was unquestionably Alfred Hitchcock, one of my true idols then and one of my most respected filmmakers now. I went to a small press luncheon with him in Boston when his movie *Frenzy* had its American premiere there in 1972. During the early part of the lunch, Hitchcock was standing and schmoozing with the assembled journalists, and instead of angling up close to him, I stayed near the table where we were going to be seated, so I could snag a seat right next to him. I succeeded, and we all talked for maybe an hour. He was as courteous and forthcoming as anyone could wish—if some inattentive person asked a question he'd just answered five minutes earlier, he smiled and patiently answered it again. I vividly remember him saying he regarded the movie *Psycho* as a comedy, a remark I've cited more than once in my writing. He really meant this, by the way. If he'd intended it to be taken seriously, he said, he would have made it in the style of a straightforward case study without all the "mysterioso touches" you see in the picture. That makes good sense to me.

Another member of the old Hollywood guard was George Cukor, whom I interviewed when the Film Society of Lincoln Center gave him a career tribute in 1979. Career tributes like this were annual publicity and fundraising events for the Society's benefit—they honored a different celebrity each year—and it was a chance for an aging veteran to get back in the public eye, however fleetingly. Cukor was eighty years old and still going strong, with a long list of major pictures in his filmography, from *Gaslight* and *The Philadelphia Story* to *A Star Is Born* and *My Fair Lady*. Many critics consider him a full-fledged auteur with a personal style, but he gave great credit to the screenwriters of his films, and for me his personal style consists largely in his emphasis on acting and dialogue.

Our conversation covered many topics, from his enormous respect for screenwriters to an "intimate thing with the camera" he saw Joan Crawford do during a shot, confirming his idea that genuine stars have a special magic when they're being photographed. I said something nice about his 1941 comedy *Two-Faced Woman*, which he considered a misfire despite Greta Garbo and Melvyn Douglas in the leads, and he stuck to his negative opinion of it, refreshingly willing to criticize his own work.

Speaking of Melvyn Douglas, a grand star of the studio era, I interviewed him when he was visiting Dartmouth College, and we talked both movies and politics. His wife of almost fifty years had been Helen Gahagan Douglas, a Congresswoman who lost a Senate election to Richard Nixon in 1950, and Melvyn was still ticked off about the smearing and Red-baiting that Nixon used to bring her down. Melvyn himself was a pioneer in escaping the sort of imprisoning contract that kept gifted artists chained to particular Hollywood studios; he had used a California peonage law to gain his freedom. He was a fine actor and a heartfelt liberal, and admirable in both departments. And speaking of Dartmouth, that's also where I interviewed Joesph Losey, another solid liberal thinker.

David Niven was another actor I enjoyed meeting. I'd always regarded him as one of the truly aristocratic screen presences, always very classy in every way. Reading his new memoir in 1975, though, I was surprised to find it full of uproariously vulgar language; he told me he didn't have an especially large vocabulary, and much of what he did have consisted of four-letter words. I agreed to interview him, and when I got off the elevator in his hotel he greeted me there and put his arm around my shoulder as we walked to his room. We had a lovely talk, and later he sent me a handwritten letter of thanks, saying it was probably illegal for an actor to write to a journalist, but he had a "sick sec," so he was doing the job himself. Like him, the note was warm and witty.

Some entertainment veterans I interviewed were specialists in musicals and comedies, including Gene Kelly, one of the most illustrious dancers and singers in film history; Donald O'Connor, the wildly inventive star of *Singin' in the Rain* and many another picture; and Ray Bolger, still most famous as the Scarecrow in *The Wizard of Oz*, although my interview was pegged to his work in Stanley Kramer's *The Runner Stumbles,* a heavily dramatic picture. "I love to learn," Bolger told me, "and I felt I would learn from a man of [Kramer's] gifts." I hope the lessons were worthwhile, because the movie is pretty bad.

And speaking of comedy, I was thrilled to interview George Burns, a superb comedian who became a favorite of mine in *The George Burns and Gracie Allen Show*, the long-running TV sitcom he did with his ditzy wife in the 1950s. The interview was a little odd because Burns fired off a joke in every sentence, and I had to keep grinning and giggling even when they weren't funny. He also used a lot of four-letter language, à la David Niven, and at the end of our talk he asked me to remove the bad words when I wrote the article, which my *Monitor* editors would have done anyway. Burns had always regarded himself as the straight man in the Burns & Allen act, but after his partner died he emerged as an excellent comic actor, making a breakthrough in 1975 with *The Sunshine Boys*, where he starred with Walter Matthau and Richard Benjamin, both of whom I also interviewed around that time.

Other iconic stars I talked with included Jack Nicholson, who was smart and articulate; Ingrid Bergman, one of the greatest Hollywood actresses; Sophia Loren, luminous on the screen and luminous in person; Kirk Douglas, a good actor and iconic star; and Gregory Peck, who was working on the fiftieth-anniversary Academy Awards ceremony and stressed the importance of honoring the technical categories by keeping those awards in the telecast despite their relative lack of glitter.

And sometimes I would interview people just because they were celebrities of the day. An example is Sylvester Stallone, who had just written and starred in *Rocky*. It's a very solid picture, and it became a huge hit, changing the movie business for a while because it made such an enormous profit on such a small investment. Stallone was perfect for the part, with the body of a boxer topped by a face that could signal sensitivity and even vulnerability; my colleague Andrew Sarris used to call him "superslob," but he was more than that in his early days. He talked to me about things like his great love for Colonial American poetry, which was probably a routine meant to give his bodybuilder physique a bit of intellectual gloss. I think he was fairly literate, but I don't think Anne Bradstreet's verse kept him up into the late night very often!

On a different note, it was fun interviewing Steve Martin, a savvy and intelligent comedian. A lesser-known figure I met by way of an interview was Paula Trueman, who had numerous movie credits including a substantial role in Clint Eastwood's western *The Outlaw Josie Wales*. She and her husband Harold Sterner, an artist and architect, became good friends.

I also remember a session with Sidney Lumet, Richard Burton, and Peter Shaffer when the film version of *Equus* came out. Other journalists were there as well, and since my own questions weren't as organized as I would have liked, I arranged a follow-up interview with Lumet, who directed the picture. What I remember most from that session is Richard Burton asking me if I was a Christian Scientist, and when I gave him a wry smile, he quoted the then-famous ad that said you didn't have to be Jewish to enjoy Levy's rye. A nice connection!

Who was the most unusual person you ever interviewed?

That depends on how you interpret "unusual," but one candidate has to be O. J. Simpson, the football star and murder suspect. He tried to get a movie career going at one point, and I had a lengthy one-on-one chat with him. The thing I remember most vividly is that he was, being a football star, a very big and imposing guy. And the thought occurred to me that this big, imposing guy could kill me in about two seconds if he wanted to. I'm not making that up! Fortunately, he didn't want to.

Truffaut and Cassavetes

I take it that many of your interviews were done more for the newspaper than for your own interests. But what were some that meant the most to you personally?

During my college years, one of the films that confirmed my interest in cinema as a serious art form was François Truffaut's masterpiece *The 400 Blows*, which had become the first real triumph of the French New Wave when it won the best director prize at Cannes in 1959. *Shoot the Piano Player* and *Jules and Jim* were also terrific, and I was eager to meet and interview Truffaut. That happened when he was in town to present *Small Change*, a fairly minor work, at the New York Film Festival in 1976. He spoke very bad English, so he was usually accompanied by his interpreter, Helen Scott, who worked with him regularly. Helen was amazing—she'd be speaking the English while he was still speaking the French—and you can see her sitting with Truffaut and Hitchcock in Truffaut's book-length interview with Hitchcock, which she very ably facilitated. What struck me was that his answers were very concise and succinct; he'd say a sentence or a few sentences and then stop. It wasn't a very conversational style, and when the interview was over I thought the questions and answers were fine, but I hadn't felt a real rapport had been struck. A little later I was walking into a screening and I heard someone calling my name—"Mr. Sterritt!"—and I looked around and there was Helen Scott, who came up to me and said Truffaut had been so impressed with our interview that he asked her to make note of my name so he could keep me in mind in the future. I was surprised, and Helen said I hadn't gone into all the "bullshit" he often got from journalists, whatever that meant. In subsequent years I did more interviews with him, and it was always the same. He was always delighted to see me, and he would answer in the same succinct way, clipped sentences with no wasted words. His English was even worse than my French, so when I saw him informally we talked haltingly or found Helen or someone nearby to translate, and he was a bit looser, a bit more conversational.

We got along so well that when he made *The Green Room*, a very unusual and enormously personal work, he didn't want to do any interviews because he felt this film reached inside his soul in such a self-revealing way—it's loosely based on Henry James's story "The Altar of the Dead," and François used it to mourn for people who had become absent from his life. I was told that he turned down an interview request from *The New York Times*, but he gave an interview to me. I don't want to give the impression I had some unique knack for getting along with important filmmakers, but Truffaut felt we had a real connection even though I wasn't sure we'd hit it off at first.

John Cassavetes was another case. I had seen and liked his first picture, *Shadows*, and I met him briefly at that time. A few years later I saw *Faces* and disliked it so much that I skipped his next two movies, *Husbands* and *Minnie and Moskowitz*. I decided to see *A Woman Under the Influence* at the 1974 New York Film Festival because I was writing about the festival for the first time and wanted to include an American entry. And it absolutely knocked me out. It was excellent but not perfect—a section in the middle of the film, about a worker injured on the job, seemed a bit disjointed—so I started calling it a deeply flawed sublime masterwork. I saw it again to confirm that it was as great as my first viewing told me, and it was, so I set up an interview with John and Gena Rowlands, who starred in the film and was John's wife and muse. His producer Sam Shaw was also there. It was a lively conversation. One item we discussed was the use of two young children in the film, which is about a construction worker and his psychologically troubled wife. In a press conference after the first festival screening, someone had asked about the kids and Cassavetes said they weren't very important to the picture, which took me aback, because I thought they provided a couple of the most striking moments—when the little girl dances in the back-yard, for instance, and when the little boy says goodnight by tenderly kissing his mother and then shaking his fist at his father, encapsulating the entire Oedipus complex in a couple of brief images. I brought that up, and John immediately backtracked on his earlier remark, saying his brain and his mouth sometimes went in different directions. His mind was as mercurial as his movies.

So we had a terrific interview, and of course I reviewed the film. My reviews were quoted in ads in *The New York Times* and elsewhere fairly often, but when *A Woman Under the Influence* had its commercial opening, a quote from my review was blazoned all over the top of the page. Cassavetes evidently took my praise seriously, and he was very hands-on with his publicity campaigns. When his next film came out, *The Killing of a Chinese Bookie*, I wasn't expecting it to be great because I've always felt that even excellent artists rarely make two masterpieces in a row. But sure enough, *The Killing of a Chinese Bookie* was another top-of-the-line achievement, very different from *A Woman Under the Influence* and wonderful on all kinds of levels. When it failed at the box office, John went back and reedited it into a shorter, tighter version, a rare occurrence for him. For me both versions are brilliant.

Some years later, a related event occurred. I joined the selection committee of the New York Film Festival, becoming one of the five people who chose the movies on the program each year. By tradition, two selections were always retrospectives, older films that hadn't previously been shown in the festival. I suggested programming a Cassavetes picture. *A Woman Under the Influence* was ineligible because the festival had already shown it, but since we all agreed on having a Cassavetes film, someone said it would be fun to ask Cassavetes for his thoughts on the subject. He had the surprising idea of showing an older film that would also be brand new: *Opening Night*, which never found an American distributor when he finished it in 1977. Now it was 1988, and this seemed like a splendid course of action.

Then I had an interesting conversation with a friend and colleague in another city who had done a great deal of major research and writing on Cassavetes and his films. I told him we wanted to put a Cassavetes movie in the festival, and he was happy to hear that, but he offered a piece of advice—don't show *Opening Night*! He said he had used it in the classroom and students were confused and alienated by it, so we should definitely stay away from that one. Little did he know that Cassavetes was suggesting exactly that film, and we went ahead with our plan. John couldn't be at the event in person because he was very sick with the liver disease that eventually killed him, and Gena stayed home with him. So I sat in the auditorium box where the filmmaker and his entourage would have been if they had been present, and from there I could look out over the whole audience throughout the screening. It was a perfect screening. Everyone was rapt with attention; they laughed in the right places and they were hushed during the dramatic scenes. You couldn't have imagined a better screening. As soon as it was over I went with Joanne Koch—she was executive director of the Film Society of Lincoln Center, the festival's parent organization—to the society office, and we telephoned John to tell him about it. He was in the shower, so we talked with Gena first, and then John came on and I told him what a superb screening it had been, which gratified him enormously. Not long afterward the film was picked up by a distributor and belatedly put into movie theaters. So we played a part in bringing that extraordinary picture back to life.

I haven't liked every Cassavetes movie, by the way. *Gloria*, for instance, is pretty weak. A very young boy has one of the leading roles in that picture, and I find his performance wooden and unconvincing; when I interviewed John around that time, I diplomatically asked how he came upon this boy and why he gave him the part. Characteristically for John, he said the boy was a *wonderful* kid, such a *nice* kid, and his family came and stayed with them and you couldn't *meet* nicer people. None of this had anything to do with acting ability, but John was a hugely intuitive filmmaker, and his intuitions didn't always serve him well. That was his personality in the proverbial nutshell, though. His last film, the appropriately named *Big Trouble*, is even worse, although it might have been less bad if Columbia Pictures hadn't butchered the final cut. That's also a rare Cassavetes film made from a screenplay by someone else, namely Andrew Bergman, who ultimately had his name taken off the movie.

But just before that John directed *Love Streams*, loosely based on a play by Ted Allan, who shares the screenplay credit with him. It's splendid in many ways, reprising some of the themes found in *A Woman Under the Influence* but with fascinating twists. Rowlands again plays a troubled woman, here named Sarah Lawson, and Cassavetes plays Robert Harmon, her alcoholic brother. The finale is wild even by Cassavetes standards: sheltering in his house during a raging storm with an assortment of barnyard animals for company, Robert finds that a naked man has abruptly materialized in his living room. Huh?! It looks as bizarre as it sounds, but to Cassavetes it's a perfectly reasonable illustration of his theory that life can give us what we really need — here it's a companion to ease loneliness and isolation—if we leave ourselves open to drastically improbable and even seemingly impossible outcomes. Cinematic storytelling doesn't get bolder or braver than this.

When someone asks me what my favorite movie is, I often name *A Woman Under the Influence*, and there's certainly no picture I love more. *The Killing of a Chinese Bookie* and *Opening Night* are very close runners-up, though, and parts of *Love Streams*, *Minnie and Moskowitz*, and some others are also superb. I have an interesting anecdote about *Opening Night*, by the way. As mentioned, Cassavetes finished it in 1977, telling the emotionally complex story of an actress, played by Rowlands, coping with age and insecurity during preview performances of a new play. Three years later, the film still hadn't had a theatrical opening. I thought the movie was marvelous, and I suggested to John that it may have simply been ahead of its time, and he should consider putting it on the market again. "Those fucking distributors," he responded with a fierce-looking smile. "They had their chance. If any museum wants a copy of that film, I'll give it to 'em, for free. Any university that wants a copy, I'll give it to 'em, for free. But those distributors can offer me anything they want, and *fuck 'em* is what I say. They had their chance, and it's too goddamn late." That sums up Cassavetes's character in all its bull-headedness and integrity.

Near the end of his life Cassavetes called me up at home one day just to talk. At one point he said he was getting near the end of his career—which was true, he died not too long afterward—and that he thought of his movies as children: some were tall and handsome, some were short and misshapen, but he loved them all. I agreed with him then and I agree with him now. Some years after that, I was invited to speak on a panel about John's films at an event in a New York theater. The other speakers included filmmaker Peter Bogdanovich, film scholar Ray Carney, Cassavetes's frequent cinematographer Al Ruban, and his old producer Sam Shaw. During the panel Sam started going on about me, saying I was John's favorite film critic. I'm not sure it's a good idea for a critic to be the favorite of a particular filmmaker, but I was flattered anyway. John was one of my favorite filmmakers and I'm glad I was his favorite too.

Spielberg, Altman, et al

Were there some major film releases that particularly caught your attention in the '70s?

One notable item was Steven Spielberg's *Jaws*, the first of the modern blockbusters. It opened in something like 2,000 theaters at once, the idea being that if you ran a huge amount of advertising and got huge audiences on the first three days, you made piles of money even if word of mouth then turned it into a flop. Before the film premiered there were many reports of terrible production difficulties involving the artificial shark and other things, but I went to the movie with an open mind, hoping Spielberg had surmounted the problems. And he had. It was an example of first-rate filmmaking craft; one of my editors once mused that entertaining is an art, and this movie proves the point. But it's also true that some of the moments audiences loved in the middle 1970s can fall flat with students today; when one of the characters tells his friends they're gonna need a bigger boat, the laughs you used to hear may not arrive. In a packed theater with a large screen it would probably work very well, but it's a kind of movie whose peak has passed. Today's mass-audience spectacles rely more on sophisticated digital trickery, and *Jaws* is a slightly different species.

I first spoke with Spielberg when *Close Encounters of the Third Kind* was opening—I also did a phone interview with J. Allen Hynek, an astronomer and UFO believer who has a cameo in the film—and I've talked with Steven on other occasions as well. I've usually held back a little with him, because I've dissed so many of his films for reflecting a twelve-year-old mind, but when he's good, as in *Jaws* and *Close Encounters of the Third Kind* and *Schindler's List*, he's splendid. We had a brief but very nice encounter when *Schindler's List* won various New York Film Critics Circle awards in 1993.

Robert Altman's *Nashville* is another kind of epic, about people rather than action or adventure or romance or melodrama. And of course it's about country music, which is hard to resist. What's most impressive is its unpredictable, almost improvisational nature, the way you can never quite tell where it's going next. And many of its performances are absolutely stellar, including scenes where actors perform songs they wrote for themselves, live before the camera, which was quite an innovation in its day. I had liked *M*A*S*H* and I greatly admired *Brewster McCloud*— although my affection for that one has cooled over the years—and some of Altman's other films are remarkable acts of imagination: *McCabe & Mrs. Miller, 3 Women, The Player*, parts of *Short Cuts*. He also made some awful pictures—*Streamers* and *Beyond Therapy* come to mind.

But while *Nashville* is the movie Bob Altman was born to make, I also need to mention *A Wedding*, another ambitious ensemble film, and a badly underrated one. The promotion for *Nashville* said it had twenty-four characters, and while some are actually minor figures with little to contribute, that's a good tagline. The ads for *A Wedding* said it had double that number, forty-eight characters, although again some are very minor. The story takes place in one vast house, and Altman handles the logistics beautifully, building a great deal of humor, sadness, and irony. And there's a scene late in the movie where the camera suddenly whips around and zooms into the eyes of a statue a couple of times. I don't think I've seen anyone comment on this, but for me, it's this moment that makes the film truly great, adding a level of mystery and ineffability that spreads its influence to every other element of the film. It's the kind of spontaneous, idiosyncratic gesture that may appeal to just one person out of a million, but in this case I'm that person. If more people noticed little moments like that, more people would appreciate this remarkable picture.

There are two basic kinds of Altman films: large-canvas movies like *Nashville* and *A Wedding* and *Short Cuts*, and smaller-canvas pictures like *Images* and *Quintet* and *Secret Honor*. And he worked outside cinema as well. I saw his production of Stravinsky's opera *The Rake's Progress* at the University of Michigan in 1982, and this was a case where my interest in music and movies were able to converge. When we talked after the performance, Bob told me he'd been pondering the idea of directing an opera, and the opportunity to direct this one plugged directly into his large-canvas mode.

In my review I described a huge metallic cobweb of scaffolds and platforms, and at some moments there were almost 150 people simultaneously onstage—grand opera indeed, and Bob told me he'd long dreamed of getting so many people onto a stage at the same time. That project came after a string of box-office disappointments had temporarily scuttled Bob's movie career and steered him toward ventures in television and theater. He managed to make a few theatrical films in the '80s, most of them based on plays and some of them as dreadful as anything he ever did. But he rebounded beautifully with *The Player* in the early '90s, and I think he could have been a successful full-time stage director if he'd so chosen.

In any case, *The Rake's Progress* wasn't as much of an anomaly as it may seem. I wrote at the time that Altman's films often have musical structures—pictures like *3 Women* and *A Wedding* are built more on evolving themes than on conventional storytelling—and I noted that the soundtracks of *Nashville* and *A Perfect Couple* are almost as tuneful as that of *Popeye*, which is a musical in the traditional sense. In our conversations he often talked about the need to experiment with new ideas and approaches; at one point he said one of the problems with filmmaking is that even the failed experiments usually have to be exposed to the public to earn back at least a fraction of their production costs, whereas painters can just stick canvases that don't work out into a closet and forget them.

I don't think any American theatrical filmmaker has surpassed Altman's spirit of adventure and willingness to take enormous artistic risks. I had quite a few conversations with him over the years. I think the first time was when he had completed *Thieves Like Us*, which wasn't taking the box office by storm, and he put the blame on Pauline Kael for calling it a "masterpiece," which he said connoted "a big heavy book you have to read in school." Our talks were too numerous for me to remember the exact circumstances—sometimes a one-on-one interview, sometimes a roundtable at a film festival. I used to coordinate film programming for the Major Speakers Series at the Makor/Steinhardt Center of the 92nd Street Y in Manhattan, where I hosted evenings with such notables as Steve Buscemi, Richard Linklater, Wim Wenders, Mary Harron, and Terry Zwigoff, and near the end of Altman's life I hosted an evening with him and Garrison Keillor talking about *A Prairie Home Companion*, his last completed film. Bob was always good humored, articulate, proud of his good movies, and refreshingly aware that he'd made some bad ones.

I should add that Altman's large-scale films had plenty of company in the 1970s, when an important development was the arrival of big semi-political epics like Michael Cimino's *The Deer Hunter*, which impressed me very much for its performances and was an extraordinary display of filmmaking craft, as in the scenes with Christopher Walken playing Russian roulette. Seeing it again more recently, though, I found parts of it discombobulated and meretricious, and I've always been suspicious of its seemingly patriotic sentiments, as when the song "God Bless America" closes the final scene. A couple of years later Cimino came out with the notorious *Heaven's Gate*, and on first viewing I found that a crashing bore. Revisiting it years later, I found it quite impressive, perhaps because my expectations were lower and I was watching it comfortably on my big flatscreen at home. Such are the little variations that can influence a critic's opinion.

Francis Ford Coppola's *Apocalypse Now* is the grandest of the '70s political pictures, and some of its performances—Marlon Brando, Robert Duvall, Martin Sheen—have made cinema history. At the time I was a little wary of a film putting so much intellectual ambition into what sometimes seems like an action picture, but now I give it credit for transcending its war-movie format. Coppola has reworked it more than once, and the longest version, *Apocalypse Now Redux*, is even more engrossing than the original. I have a lot of respect for it, even though some of the people involved in it—the screenwriter John Milius in particular—have politics very unlike my own. I interviewed Coppola when *One from the Heart* was about to have its first big screening in Radio City Music Hall, and when another journalist asked how he would know if it went over successfully, he good-naturedly said that when 5,000 people in a room are not having a good time, you will know it! The film didn't prove popular—it pretty much bankrupted American Zoetrope, his studio—and he started making projects motivated more by commercial potential than personal expression. Later he turned to small-scale productions with more personal leanings, none of which I find especially memorable, and in 2024 he finished his long-dreamed of megaproject, *Megalopolis*, which is quite a mess, in my view. In the meanwhile, his faith in *One from the Heart* hasn't wavered. As for me, I was unmoved by it then and I'm unmoved by it now. Francis loves it, and when I interviewed his daughter Sofia years later, she said she loves it too. Good for them, but I don't share the sentiment.

Inventive Independents

I know you've been interested in many smaller, independently made films. Talk about some of them from the 1970s and 1980s.

Ralph Bakshi is a lesser figure who made his name in the animation field, where he pursued an earnest campaign to bring X-rated content to movie cartoons. His breakthrough film was *Fritz the Cat*, which I don't like at all, and his next features, *Heavy Traffic* and *Coonskin*, push the bad-taste envelope even further. Then he turned to a different kind of fantasy in *Wizards*, and when I met him he was making his adaptation of *The Lord of the Rings*, decades before Peter

Jackson's overblown version of the J. R. R. Tolkien books. We had a good talk, and I remember his studio being positively littered with hobbit materials. When the film finally opened, it was a real disappointment. He was using the rotoscoping technique, which calls for tracing cartoon images over photographed footage. But quite a bit of live-action material was visible in the final cut because he ran out of time and/or money before the rotoscoping was complete.

Bakshi's subsequent career was also disappointing, although I'm very fond of *American Pop*, a sort of valentine to the so-called love generation. The most memorable thing he told me was that one of his favorite artists was Norman Rockwell, famed for his wholesome-as-apple-pie paintings in mass-market magazines. I expressed my surprise at hearing this from the maker of *Fritz the Cat* and *Coonskin*, so he showed me a Rockwell picture or two, saying such effects could only be done in painting, and Rockwell had done it masterfully. Very interesting. I wouldn't have expected such a strenuously transgressive animator to harbor a love of Norman Rockwell, but the unexpected happens now and then. This reminds me of my surprise when Woody Allen said one of his comic heroes is Bob Hope, of all people.

I definitely want to mention Martin Brest, who has completely vanished from the scene. In 1977 he made *Hot Tomorrows*, a small independent feature made at the American Film Institute, which asserted proprietorship and wouldn't allow it to be released commercially, even though David Lynch managed to get *Eraserhead* into extremely wide release, where it remains to this day. The main characters of *Hot Tomorrows* are a pair of displaced New Yorkers in California, one of whom is forever mooning about the impermanence of human existence; eventually the other is killed in an accident, only to come bouncing back to life in a hugely imaginative finale with the title song from the 1930s classic *42nd Street* on the soundtrack while the Grim Reaper and assorted corpses do a wild dance involving coffins—it's one part Busby Berkeley, one part Charles Addams, and utterly original, unlike anything I've seen before or since, beautifully realized on what was obviously a shoestring budget.

I saw *Hot Tomorrows* at some independent film series or festival, and I thought it was absolutely sensational, a tale of death and death-related things told with great liveliness and humor. It's a narrative movie that cracks off into another dimension, as Brest put it in one of my conversations with him, adding that the pitch-dark side of the *42nd Street* theme is hard to miss if you really listen. Not surprisingly, one of Marty's favorite films was *The Cremator*, the great Czechoslovak film by Juraj Herz, which also shoots away into a different dimension. In order to get *Hot Tomorrows* into production, Brest submitted a brief "dummy" script for AFI approval. The actual screenplay was written backwards—he started with the ending and then figured out a story that could come in front of it; the idea was to make a movie where things are reversed and then the reversal is reversed, although that description makes the film sound trickier than it is. After leaving the AFI he came to believe it was a useful institution, but he wasn't crazy about the place when he was there—what he expected was the Bauhaus of film, or a 1920s Paris where intellectuals spend their evenings arguing new concepts in cinema, but what he found was closer to a school for insurance salesmen. Still and all, he used its resources to make a unique movie that deserves far more prominence than it has.

In subsequent years Marty showed his versatility. He made the superb comedy *Going in Style*, another scandalously overlooked picture, and *Beverly Hills Cop*, a huge Eddie Murphy hit. When that film opened I asked him if it was an Eddie Murphy movie rather than a Martin Brest movie, and he pointed to some elements that he felt were his own touches, which seemed reasonable to me. *Midnight Run* was an interesting Hollywood production, and *Scent of a Woman* won an Academy Award for Al Pacino, an Oscar nomination for best picture, and nominations for Marty's directing and Bo Goldman's screenplay. But the ambitious *Meet Joe Black*, a takeoff on the classic *Death Takes a Holiday* idea, was overlong and overblown, and then a dismally received romantic comedy ended his directorial career. I suppose he's alive and well out there somewhere, but he hasn't been heard from in quite a while.

And then there's David Lynch, who made his feature debut with *Eraserhead*, another AFI anomaly. When it first became a phenomenon on the midnight movie circuit, I was leading a very busy life and wasn't really up for midnight movies. In my Boston days I had gone to many midnight avant-garde film showings when a theater manager I knew was programming them in his commercial moviehouse, but those days were behind me, so I didn't see *Eraserhead* at first. Then a French filmmaker recommended it to me as a very advanced piece of work, and I found that it was playing during the day at a small Long Island theater, so I took myself off to see it. I was genuinely impressed. It was completely original, unlike anything I had seen before— unlike anything *anybody* had seen before—and a true work of imagination, beautifully realized in almost every respect, despite its obviously bare-bones budget.

I have a funny memory about that first viewing. In the last shot of the movie, the main character, Henry, and a secondary character, the Lady in the Radiator, embrace each other with great affection, and the image is deliberately overexposed, so everything seems almost blindingly bright. At the little Long Island theater, the projection was so bad that the final image barely registered on the screen—there was *something* there, and it seemed to be moving, but you couldn't make out what it was. I thought that was a great touch for the finale of this completely unconventional film, but when I saw it again under better circumstances, I saw that the shot was completely legible. I still think the inscrutable image would have been a more radical ending, and maybe a better one! That aside, *Eraserhead* still stands as one of the boldest films in American cinema.

I first met David when he made *Dune* a few years later. Before that he'd done *The Elephant Man*, which was produced by none other than Mel Brooks, who had loved *Eraserhead*, and I was extremely impressed by how much of the *Eraserhead* sensibility Lynch had managed to smuggle into this Hollywood production. He made *Dune* as part of a deal where he would make one big movie for the producer and then a smaller movie for himself: the big movie was *Dune*, the smaller one was *Blue Velvet*. He wasn't nearly as well known then as he soon became, so I asked him about his early work and learned about his background, especially his years as an art student, when moving from the Midwest to Philadelphia revealed the ugliness of the world to him. He was an affable and articulate interlocutor, and we had a number of talks over the years.

One memorable conversation was at Cannes, when *Mulholland Dr.* was shown in 1999. By then David seemed more eccentric, talking around things rather than directly at things—not evasive, just vague in his thinking, or at least in the way he put that thinking into words. But he had always been an odd communicator. When we had our very first conversation, he had another project called "Ronnie Rocket" waiting to go if he could get the money for it. I asked what it would be about, and he seemed to struggle to find words, and finally he said, "He's real short." That was all! And it was like that when we talked about *Mulholland Dr.* He said quite a lot, but he seemed to be floating off in his own mental space. I had just seen *Mulholland Dr.* for the first time and hadn't had time think about it, so near the end of the interview I brought up its very puzzling structure and asked whether it would make perfect sense if I sat down and considered it in an organized way. He said yes. Then I asked the same question about an earlier film, *Lost Highway*, and he smiled and said no. And one of the things I love about Lynch's best work is that it's so purely intuitive. You can't always tell whether it makes sense, but in the long run that doesn't really matter because the images and the sounds are the whole point. He once told me that when he had been a young painter, he often wished some little noise could accompany a particular painting. Making movies was with his way of having that come true.

Roger Corman was a different kind of independent filmmaker—in fact, he became such a powerful force in independent films that he was an institution in himself. I found him to be a lovely guy, very pleasant and informative. Back in 1962 he had directed *The Intruder*, a film attacking racial segregation in the South, written by Charles Beaumont and starring William Shatner a few years before the *Star Trek* juggernaut. The picture had failed with audiences and lost money, and Corman had vowed not let this happen again. By the time I interviewed him in the '70s, he took pride in making pictures that had constructive messages embedded in their stories but didn't alienate viewers by pushing the messages too obviously. As he put it in our 1979 interview, his films were "very committed—personally, psychologically, and politically," but he was "very careful to make this a subtextual commitment," allowing audiences "to see a commercially oriented film, and find to their surprise... that there is more there." He pointed to the recently released *Piranha*, directed by Joe Dante from a screenplay by John Sayles, as an example, since it had a progressive perspective on environmental matters. I took Roger's point, but I didn't think *Piranha* was very good as a movie, so we had a pleasant difference of opinion about that.

Anyone who directs dozens of features and produces hundreds of them is bound to have an uneven filmography, and Corman has made his share of stinkers, but he's also done some truly sensational pictures. *X: The Man with the X-Ray Eyes* is an example of his finest work, inventive and intelligent from start to finish. I also admire *The Premature Burial* and *The Masque of the Red Death*, two of the best entries in his Edgar Allan Poe cycle. He enabled many gifted newcomers to launch their directing careers—Scorsese, Coppola, Dante, Demme, and so on. And later he distributed films by the likes of Truffaut, Fellini, Kurosawa, and Bergman to American theaters. He spent decades making low-budget pictures with a little intelligence, and sometimes a lot of intelligence, that have pleased enormous numbers of people at theaters and drive-ins around the world. He's often been called the King of the Bs, but that lighthearted label doesn't capture the full measure of his long and worthwhile career.

International figures

You've been speaking mainly of Americans so far, but I know you've ranged much farther afield.

The front page of the *Monitor* used to say "An International Daily Newspaper," and one of the editions—back then there were five editions a day, six days a week—was printed in London and aimed at European readers. So we tried not to be too parochial, although most of our readers were American and the editors favored American subjects. That said, I wrote as much about European and Asian film as I could get away with, and Latin American and Middle Eastern cinema as well.

This worked best when an overseas filmmaker had a substantial American presence as well as a global audience. A good Exhibit A is the phenomenal Akira Kurosawa, the Japanese titan I interviewed when his epic *Kagemusha* came to US theaters in 1980. He spoke in Japanese, and the interpreter was Audie Bock, who was translating his autobiography into English at the time. *Kagemusha* is a period drama set in the sixteenth century, but Kurosawa saw it as an implicit commentary on the dangers of rigidity in civic life.

Few filmmakers have Kurosawa's exalted status, of course, and I've certainly interviewed lesser lights, such as the Brazilian filmmaker Carlos Diegues, who talked about the importance of entertaining audiences and the value of movies for raising social awareness, and the Chilean director Rolando Klein, whose *Chac*, about the rain ceremony of a drought-stricken village, had its US premiere in 1977, and it might deserve reviving now, when there is much more awareness of climate problems and of indigenous peoples— the actors are indigenous nonprofessionals and the dialogue is spoken in Tzeltal and Mayan dialects. But back to world-class filmmakers. In the '70s the Italian writer-director Lina Wertmuller scored arthouse hits with *The Seduction of Mimi* and *Love and Anarchy* and *Swept Away*. Those are the shorthand titles of the films—long, wordy titles were one of her trademarks, so the full monikers are *Mimi the Metalworker*, *Wounded in Honor* and *Film of Love and Anarchy, or Rather: This Morning at 10, in Via dei fiore, in the Well-Known Brothel...* and *Swept Away by an Unusual*

Destiny in the Blue Sea of August. I interviewed her when the first-rate *Seven Beauties* (aka *Pasqualino Sevenbeauties*) had its American opening, and I spoke with her again when *A Night Full of Rain* (aka *The End of the World in Our Usual Bed on a Night Full of Rain*) came along. The latter was poorly received by critics, ending what was supposed to be a multifilm contract with Warner Bros. and putting the brakes on what had been a steady rise for her. I asked her how an outspoken socialist could collaborate with a flagrantly capitalistic Hollywood studio, and she said that when you live in the jungle you need to play by jungle rules—not the most persuasive explanation I can imagine. She continued making films, but her glory days were behind her.

Agnès Varda, on the other hand, was principled to her bones. I first met her in 1978 and got to know her better when I worked with the New York Film Festival a decade later. She was as warm, savvy, and unsentimental as her best pictures. Some of her work comes close to avant-garde cinema, and she also made a great many documentaries—in short, she was a hugely versatile talent who had lasting success in the scandalously male-dominated field of cinema.

Her first major film, *Cleo from 5 to 7*, was one of the early-'60s masterpieces—along with early features by Truffaut, Godard, Resnais, and Rivette—that got me enthusiastic about art movies in general and French movies in particular. The title character is a young singer who's waiting for the results of a medical test to find out whether she has cancer, and in the opening scene she's consulting with a tarot-card reader who sees doom in her future but doesn't reveal it to her. The rest of the story shows her doing ordinary things—shopping, chatting, sitting in a café, getting visits from her lover and her songwriter, and finally striking up a spontaneous friendship with a soldier about to leave for the Algerian War, which looms in the background of the picture. It's a charming film, romantic and unsentimental at once, and superbly acted by Corinne Marchand and everyone else, including the great cinema composer Michel Legrand, who plays the songwriter.

Agnès loved to experiment, and while I'm not very fond of *Les Créatures* and the California-made *Lions Love (... and Lies)*, which strain too hard to be odd and quirky, *One Sings, the Other Doesn't* has many fine moments and *Vagabond* is simply magnificent, utterly human and profoundly compassionate throughout. Her career was long, varied, and distinguished, and I'm proud to have known her.

I know the French New Wave has been important to you.

It definitely has, and I've had the opportunity to meet and talk with each core member of the New Wave group—Godard, Rivette, Rohmer, Chabrol, and especially Truffaut—and also key figures in the Left Bank Group, including Varda and Resnais, both towering figures. I also interviewed Marguerite Duras, the great writer and intensely avant-garde filmmaker, who told me about her efforts to establish *le cinéma différent* as an alternative to conventional cinema. She had a feisty personality, and when I asked her about something she'd said at a recent press conference, she denied saying it and wouldn't budge on the matter when I pressed it. Fortunately, her interpreter was in the room, and after the session she assured me that Marguerite had indeed said exactly what I thought she'd said. But it was fun talking with that gifted and eccentric artist. And by the way, our interview was at something like 10:30 in the morning and Marguerite was drinking scotch, which might explain her lapse of memory about the press conference!

Jazz

You've also written a lot about music and musicians. Tell me more about that.

I've already mentioned the minimalist music I was turning into a specialty, but I also wrote a fair amount about jazz and did quite a number of interviews with jazz musicians, from the flutist Hubert Laws to Phil Woods, the reed player and bandleader. Playing piano in my high-school dance band had given me a lasting affection for big-band jazz, so it was fun to sit down with people like Woody Herman and Maynard Ferguson, major veterans of the swing era. Woody was full of enthusiasm for Alan Broadbent, an arranger he was working with. I told Alan about this when I met him socially later on, and he was very surprised that Woody had mentioned him at all. George Shearing was another giant. He had been blind from birth, and he insisted that blindness hadn't had the slightest effect on his life or his work, except that it might have been one reason he gravitated toward music. I asked him if it was true, as legend had it, that he wrote his all-time biggest hit, "Lullaby of Birdland," in fifteen minutes. He said it was indeed true—he had written it at his house in New Jersey while having a steak in his dining room. But, he added, it was actually fifteen minutes plus the thirty years he'd been in the business!

Some of the musicians I interviewed were stars of the moment—Chuck Mangione, Chick Corea—rather than people I personally listened to a lot. Also in the mix was Buell Neidlinger, a tremendously versatile bassist who worked with the avant-garde jazz pianist Cecil Taylor and played in the Boston Symphony Orchestra as well. I talked with him in his apartment in Boston, but he immediately pulled out a box full of psychedelic smokables, and from there the conversation didn't develop in a very lucid way, so I never wrote the article. I remember Buell doing a recital in one of the smaller Boston concert venues, playing classical bass viol for the first half and then returning after intermission with rock'n'roll on an electric bass—a delightful surprise, since in those days the rock and classical worlds were more separated than they are now.

Other jazz interviewees were people whose music and fame were everywhere, such as Max Roach, the towering bop drummer, and Michel Legrand, one of the great movie composers. But my interview with Dave Brubeck really stands out for me. I had discovered his music when I was in high school, and some albums of the '50s and '60s were favorites of mine—*Time Out* and *Time Further Out*, where he made terrific innovations in jazz time signatures, and *The Dave Brubeck Quartet at Carnegie Hall*, a superb live recording. And I'd seen him and his quartet in concert. Our interview was set for a restaurant near the concert hall, and when he arrived he told me he'd just discovered that the sound system at the hall had been set up all wrong. He had to fix the problem right away, but he could spare fifteen or twenty minutes, and I thought a good, concentrated session would probably work. So we started talking, and it was excellent—he was intelligent, articulate, and focused, getting the point of every question every time and giving concise answers without ever seeming rushed or superficial. Quite a performance! One detail I remember is that his family was very important to him, and he mentioned one of his grandchildren. I remembered a piece on one of his albums dedicated to that grandchild, "Charles Matthew Hallelujah," and when I mentioned this he was delighted that I made the connection. Then he scurried back to fix the sound problem.

After my article ran I received a handwritten thank-you letter—a real letter, not just a note—from Dave saying how much he'd enjoyed the interview. Then a couple of weeks later I received a second hand-written letter from Dave thanking me again. I wasn't sure whether to be pleased or not: maybe he'd enjoyed the interview so much that he felt compelled to write me two letters, or maybe he simply forgot he had written the first one. But it was a nice gesture either way.

My interview with the great alto saxophone player Cannonball Adderley also had an interesting aftermath. We were set to talk between sets at a Boston jazz club, and watching him during the first set made me nervous. When he talked to the audience, he put on a jazzman-jive accent that I could hardly understand, full of slurred words, mumbled slang, and hipster inflections. This interview might not be easy! After the set I made my way toward the dressing room, and Cannonball was waiting for me in the corridor, and he ushered me into the room. And all the jive talk and all the slurred words were gone! He was completely articulate and completely professional, and he had a ready answer to every question. Then he went back onstage and it was all hipster talk again. Cannonball was quite the showman.

A few days later I was home on a weekend afternoon, and the phone rang, and the caller introduced himself as Cannonball Adderley's father. He had seen my article reprinted in one of the local newspapers that carried the *Monitor* News Service—he lived in Florida—and he wanted to thank me for writing this lovely interview with his son. Then after a few minutes he said, "Now Cannonball's ma would like to talk with you," and sure enough, Mrs. Adderley came on the line. They were both quite thrilled, and I can't imagine why, because Cannonball was one of the most famous jazz musicians in America, perhaps in the world, and I'm sure there'd been many interviews with him over the years. Maybe it was just the fun of seeing him in their hometown paper. In the interview, by the way, I asked Cannonball how he acquired his nickname. He chuckled and said other kids called him Cannibal because of his weight. "I always did like to eat," he explained.

Popstars

I also interviewed some pop singers. One of the biggest was Marc Bolan, of T. Rex fame, and he was terrific, a nice, smiling guy full of energy that I tried to capture in my article, which one of my more benighted editors made drastically shorter because Marc was too androgynous for him. Another star was Peggy Lee, a terrific singer, although she was past her prime when we spoke in 1975. I had a fun experience with the Rolling Stones when one of their concert films was released. I was invited to a big dinner bash—at the Tavern on the Green, or some such high-toned venue—and the publicist said I could bring along both my kids. But when we arrived, there were just two tickets, not the three I'd arranged for. The person at the door agreed to straighten things out, but it took several minutes, during which a flood of people were arriving, and I figured that by the time we finally entered we'd have the most faraway table in the place. Sure enough, the main room was full and they shunted us into another room on the side. Which was also where they put the Stones, it turned out. They were at the table right next to ours, or rather three of them were, since only four were at the event and Charlie Watts was at his own table in the main room. I leaned over and started a conversation, and the rock'n'rollers were delighted to talk. When my kids got bored, they picked up a bunch of the printed programs and scurried from one Stone to another getting autographs and then going back for more, of which they accumulated quite a stack. A great evening.

Over in the country-music area, I talked with Tanya Tucker, and more memorably with Johnny Cash when he was in Philadelphia for a concert. I'll also mention Helen Reddy and the superstar Linda Ronstadt, after a concert on Long Island not far from where I lived. She came into her dressing room with her makeup off and cold cream on her face, and she truly looked like a girl next door who'd just gotten off from work. She turned out to be a nonstop talker and it was all I could do to keep up with her. Good fun. And although I didn't interview Bob Dylan, a friend and I met him backstage at a concert in the Boston area when he was just starting out. It was a fleeting encounter, but he answered most pleasantly when I asked if he wrote "Masters of War," one of that era's most hard-hitting protest songs.

Covering rock and pop gave me the perk of free concert tickets, and I had the good fortune to see Elvis Presley, the Rolling Stones, Pink Floyd, and plenty of other great groups and singers, some of whom, like Alice Cooper and the J. Geils Band, were enormous fun to watch as well as listen to. One experience I had was pure '60s in an unpleasant way, though. I showed up at the Boston Garden for a Jimi Hendrix show and my press ticket hadn't been held at the proper window for pickup. As I went to another window to straighten things out, a cop yelled at me to leave—the show was about to start and they were clearing out loiterers in the lobby. I ignored the cop and commenced explaining the situation to the supervisor in the ticket window, whereupon the cop came at me, grabbed me, dragged me across the lobby, and threw me out the door. So much for that concert.

The next day I told my editor what had happened, and he was outraged—this was a textbook example of the prejudice against young people held by too many older people in that age-polarized decade. The editor asked me to write a memo describing the incident. Then the *Monitor* complained to the Boston Police Department, and they sent a representative to apologize. As we sat and talked to him, he started the colloquy by asking me, "Did you have those chin-whiskers at the time?" Of course I'd had my little beard—this whole thing had happened about two days earlier—and this cop evidently saw my chin-whiskers as an explanation for the other cop's behavior. In any case, that was one concert that didn't get covered by the *Monitor*!

Not every interview I did was smooth sailing, either. A rough one was my interview with Rahsaan Roland Kirk, who was famous for playing two or three wind instruments at once, including obscure, exotic instruments like the manzello and the stritch. I interviewed him at the Berklee College of Music, a well-known Boston school. Rahsaan was blind, so I told him I'd be recording the interview, and he didn't object. Two or three Berkeley students came over to listen, and they started interjecting questions that weren't very interesting—when did you switch from this drummer to that drummer, and the like—so it was a little difficult to keep the flow of the conversation going. When the interview came to an end, Rahsaan surprised me by asking me to give him the tape I had recorded. I told him I needed the tape to write my article. But he insisted that I had to hand it over then and there. I asked why, and he said, "Because I'm no fool!" in a very aggrieved way. Nothing like this had happened to me before, and I wasn't sure what to do. I was about to give him the tape and forget about the article, but I tried one more time, asking if I could take the tape for now and mail it to him afterward. He reluctantly agreed and I got out of there. I don't think I wrote the article and I don't think I mailed him the tape.

That's how different these sessions could be. Dave Brubeck writes you thank-you letters, Cannonball Adderley's mom and dad call you up, and Rahsaan Roland Kirk doesn't want you to leave the room with the tape in your possession. Go figure.

AVANT-GARDE FILMMAKERS

Tell about your longtime interest in avant-garde cinema.

When I first started reading about film I'd see discussions of movies like Luis Buñuel's *Un Chien andalou* and *L'Âge d'or*, and when I first saw *Film Culture* magazine I found out about Kenneth Anger, Jack Smith, Andy Warhol, and people like that. I was curious about what these films might actually be like. Earlier I said that seeing *Last Year at Marienbad* was one of the things that got me enthusiastic about movies in the first place, because it was like hearing a language I never knew existed and wanted to understand, and it was very much the same with avant-garde film, or experimental film, as it was more often called in those days.

It was hard to see these movies, since they were noncommercial and nontheatrical by definition. But when I was in college, Fred Camper, who became a very good friend, was running the MIT Film Society, right across the river from Boston University where I was going. He showed a lot of independent and avant-garde and experimental film, so I made many a trip over there. I think that's where I saw my first movies by Stan Brakhage, Bruce Conner, Larry Jordan, and various others; not all of them were great, but the best of them were marvelous. One particular experience I remember was seeing *The Art of Vision*, a Brakhage film—silent, like almost all his films—that runs for about four and a half hours. So I have to thank Fred for a tremendous amount of my early education in that area of cinema.

When I came to New York it was possible to see a good deal more, occasionally at the New York Film Festival and more frequently at places like Anthology Film Archives and the Collective for Living Cinema and the Millennium Film Workshop, although I can't remember the first times that I went to those particular establishments. Anthology was run by the legendary Jonas Mekas, who I got to know pretty well. When I first went there it was housed in a small screening room on Wooster Street, and Jonas was raising money for a more elaborate home; it was amusing to sit on a folding chair in the little Wooster Street place and hear Jonas's tape-recorded pitch for money to help him raise the millions of dollars he needed. Eventually he did open a much grander venue on the corner of Second Avenue and 2nd Street in the East Village, complete with a research library and other amenities. The core of the programming was the so-called Essential Cinema collection, but they showed all sorts of other items, including commercial Hollywood movies. It's been a terrific resource for decades.

What was Jonas Mekas like?

I knew him for decades. He was a lovely guy, but he'd stop at nothing — or at very little — to promote the movies he cared about. Here's an example. When I was hunting out avant-garde movies for the New York Film Festival, someone suggested we consider Peter Emmanuel Goldman's avant-garde feature *Echoes of Silence*, made about twenty-five years earlier. It's a film I already knew and liked, but the other committee members weren't convinced and we didn't select it. Not long afterward I heard Jonas give a talk somewhere, and he came up with a wild story. He said he'd been the person who recommended the film, which may have been true, but then he claimed that whatever committee member he'd spoken to had asked if he'd shown the film at Anthology, and if so, how many people were in the audience. Only a few people were in the audience, Jonas allegedly replied, whereupon the committee member allegedly said the NYFF couldn't possibly show such an unpopular movie. Nonsense! I'd bet the farm that no such conversation ever took place.

Another example of Jonas's persistence happened when my son Craig and I were leaving an Anthology screening. The next show scheduled for that day was devoted to a new genre Jonas and company had cooked up — the "three-shot film," made by filmmakers who were free to interpret "three shots" any way they liked, using a total of three shots, or using three shots multiple times in different configurations, or whatever. This didn't sound particularly promising to me, and Craig and I were heading for home. But Jonas lost no time in buttonholing me and delivering a spiel. This is a groundbreaking event! Nothing like this has ever been done before! Would you turn down the chance to hear the first sonnets ever written? Okay, okay, I said, and we walked back into the auditorium. And as I expected, the films were mildly interesting at best, and a trailblazing new genre was not being born. I'll give Craig the last word about this: one of the films consisted of three shots culled from some obscure porn movie, repeated over and over, and Craig leaned over and said, "This must be the first limerick." Touché!

Were there other places showing avant-garde films?

Not many, but even in Boston there were some. One interesting place was the Kenmore Square Theater, managed by a wonderful guy named Roger Stevens, who started programming all kinds of movies in addition to the regular commercial films that were the theater's main business. He showed family films and classic films on weekends, and he started showing avant-garde movies at midnight on weekends. He pitched them as underground movies, things you would never see by the light of day in an ordinary theater. And he showed some pretty adventurous things. That was where I first saw Warhol's *My Hustler* and Cassavetes's great film *Shadows*. Roger even showed Michael Snow's *Wavelength*, which I regard as one of the greatest movies ever made but is so demanding that most people have trouble sitting through five minutes of it. I went there regularly and got to know Roger well. And in the meanwhile I'd go over to MIT where my friend Fred Camper showed even more unconventional and daring stuff. The main avant-garde showplaces in New York were Anthology Film Archives, the Collective for Living Cinema, curated by knowledgeable folks like Simon Field and Alf Bold, and the Millennium Film Workshop, run by Howard Guttenplan. All worthwhile venues.

Did you write about avant-garde film very often?

As often as I could. One reason was my personal interest. Another was the fact that the artists in this very noncommercial field are often struggling for financing and for audiences, and I wanted to support their efforts. Then too, there was a certain amount of interest in it among the general public, especially when an enterprising exhibitor promoted it as "underground" moviemaking, which gave a sort of cachet, making it sound like something transgressive and exciting and adventurous. So sometimes I felt I was reaching at least a small number of interested readers. Of course, the *Monitor* editors resisted this sort of thing—it was a general-interest newspaper and they wanted me to write about the big movies with the big ads in *The New York Times* and the *Boston Globe*, not these obscure things that nobody ever heard of. But I stuck to my guns and got as much into the paper as I had time to write and I could persuade them to publish.

Stan Brakhage was the first major avant-garde filmmaker I interviewed. He was doing a show at a library on Long Island, not far from where I lived at the time, so I met him there, we had lunch together, and then I drove him to the airport for his flight back to Colorado, where he lived in the mountains with his family. At lunch another major avant-gardist joined us: Ed Emshwiller, who also lived on Long Island, so I got to know him too. We talked for quite a long while, and I felt like I was getting into that circle a bit for the first time. I kept up my acquaintance with Stan over the years and always found him an incredibly articulate filmmaker and a very warm person; he had a reputation for being prickly and egotistical, and I'm sure he was, but I saw very little of that. We met many times over the years, including an onstage interview I did with him at the Telluride Film Festival, and he was always a pleasure to be with.

I'll mention another amusing thing—a TV show I was on many times was a CNBC program called *America After Dark*, where my friend and critical colleague Thelma Adams and I would talk about new mainstream releases. One night when I got home after one of these appearances my phone rang and it was Stan Brakhage, gushing about how fascinating I'd been and how glad he was that I said something or other. What amused me about this was that Stan was a super intellectual who made completely noncommercial, non-narrative movies, and here he was watching *America After Dark* and being so thrilled with whatever it was I said that he had to phone me and tell me right away. Surprising, but sweet.

In later years I did many interviews with avant-garde filmmakers and it was almost always interesting, although I remember that Bruce Conner—one of my very favorites, for the sheer joy of watching his movies—turned out to be pretty boring, talking about picayune details like how he had gotten the preexisting footage he used in this or that movie. Part of the fascination of avant-garde cinema—and the same thing goes for avant-garde theater, avant-garde music, and so forth—is the need to figure out what the person is trying to accomplish before going on to evaluate whether it succeeds or not, so it was always illuminating to talk with these filmmakers and find out what they felt they were doing. Some of them became really close friends. Ernie Gehr is a wonderful filmmaker who is very rigorous in his work but is a very warm and personable individual. He used to stay at my apartment when he came to New York. Another was Warren Sonbert, a really wonderful filmmaker who was also a guest at my place in Lower Manhattan.

A couple of experiences with those two stand out for me, both connected to the New York Film Festival, where I did a lot of work in the annual avant-garde film program. One year we were having trouble coming up with a movie to fill out the show, and we learned that Ernie had a new movie called *Side/Walk/Shuttle*. He was a very demanding filmmaker whose movies were not all that audience friendly, but this turned out to be a delightful work that he'd filmed going up and down in the elevator of a building in San Francisco with his camera; a guard had told him he wasn't allowed to do that, so he was not only filming the material for this wonderful movie, he was doing it while hiding his camera from view. Quite an accomplishment.

We showed one of Warren's movies during my first year on the selection committee and it didn't go over all that well. Warren's work was very non-linear and non-narrative, and he almost always made silent films, and in a big auditorium like Alice Tully Hall, where most of the festival movies were shown, it was difficult to hold an audience's attention with a completely silent film. The screening went okay, but it didn't go beautifully. And the next year Warren shifted gears and made a sound film—not a movie with sync sound like a Hollywood film, but a movie with an expressive music track. It was called *Friendly Witness*, and to this day I think it's one of the greatest films he ever made, and it went over splendidly at the festival. Then he made another film with a fine music track, *Short Fuse*, but while I loved it, some other members of the committee—there were five of us—wouldn't go along with it, so it was rejected until the following year, when the committee had a slightly different membership and it was accepted and screened. Warren was a very close friend until his death from AIDS, and shortly before he died he was planning to do some filming at my son Jeremy's loft, a few minutes from my place. I wish that had happened.

I've already mentioned Michael Snow, one of the greatest. I spoke with him more than once, including a lengthy interview that shortages of time and space prevented from getting into print. Not all of his films resonate with me, but *Wavelength* is masterpiece, a word I don't use lightly. It's around forty-five minutes long, and it's basically a very slow zoom across a mostly empty room. At first you see the whole room, which is a typical loft in downtown Manhattan, and as the zoom proceeds, ever so gradually, the field of vision shrinks, and at the end of the film the zoom has zeroed in on a photograph tacked to the opposite wall, showing waves on the open sea, and the photo fills the entire screen. So you've progressed from seeing everything, i.e. the whole room, to seeing very little, i.e. a single still photo— but in a way you're seeing more than ever, since it's a photo of the boundless sea, although only one bounded portion is visible, so the vision is still delimited and controlled. There's also a soundtrack, consisting mainly of a sine wave rising from very low pitch to very high pitch. And a few things happen along the way—a couple of women carry a piece of furniture into the loft, a man staggers in and collapses on the floor, and one of the women returns, finds him, and calls a friend who evidently calls the police, because at the very end the sine wave is joined by sounds of sirens.

When I show *Wavelength* to students, I tell them that when they realize they're in for a single slow zoom, their hearts will sink—is it *all* going to be like this?—and the answer will be yes and no. Yes, because it's a single zoom in a single location, but no, because other things also happen. In addition to the human activities, the zoom shot is more complicated than a simplistic description makes it sound—the zoom moves sporadically, with many hitches and stutters, and the color frequently changes as different filters are placed over the lens, and there's also a flashback to an earlier point in the shot. There's really a lot to look at. One of my Columbia students—Rahul Hamid, who became a good friend, worked as an editor at *Cineaste*, and died tragically young—saw it for the first time in my class and said he was surprised by how action-packed it was! I truly love it for both its physical manifestations and its metaphysical implications. The first time I talked with Snow I asked why the zoom proceeds so unevenly, since it should have been easy to get a smooth, even motion, and also why the filters are placed over the lens in such an obvious and visible way. He said he wanted the film to look like what it is, a humanly made work, not an impersonal product of machinery and equipment.

Some time later I had my first interview with Steve Reich, the great composer. I asked why he rarely used electronic devices to create and realize his music, which is immaculately precise and regular. He said the music needed to have a human dimension, and he illustrated the point in a marvelously clear way: generate a tone with an electronic gizmo, reproduce it on an oscilloscope, and you'll see a perfectly smooth wave; then have a virtuoso violinist play it as smoothly and cleanly as possible, and no matter how well the virtuoso does it, you'll see the wave jumping all over the place. I thought this was a fine musical analogue for what Snow had said about his visuals, and when I said this to Steve, he reached over and pulled out an album of his I didn't yet have in my own collection—it was *Four Organs* and *Phase Patterns* on the Shandar label—and the image on the album jacket was the last image of *Wavelength*! Steve then informed me that Michael was a close friend and that *Wavelength* was as great a film as he'd ever seen. I found this a lovely confluence of my musical and cinematic interests.

Turning to Kenneth Anger, it took me quite a while to catch up with him in person. His classic *Scorpio Rising* was a legendary work from the moment it premiered, and it got major notoriety in the '60s when a theater manager was arrested for showing it, although by today's standards it's very mild in the transgression department.

He made other brilliant works as well—*Fireworks*, *Eaux d'artifice*, and the two versions of *Rabbit's Moon* are my favorites—but for some reason I didn't meet him for a long time, even when someone I knew was squiring him around a film festival. So it was a surprise when I got a call asking if I'd like Kenneth Anger to come and speak to the avant-garde film class I was teaching at Columbia. This came out of the clear blue sky, and I was delighted to accept. Then it turned out that Kenneth also needed someone to put him up during his New York visit. He had little money and lived very frugally, and while he had a couple of possible places to stay, he was looking for something a little better. Unfortunately, I was getting divorced at the time, and I had temporarily moved to an apartment smaller than my usual one, so I couldn't accommodate him. But he came and visited my class anyway, and he gave a great talk, mainly about his films but also about the mystical practices—he was a follower of the occultist Aleister Crowley—that were a big part of his life. The only drawback was that he wanted me to show *Inauguration of the Pleasure Dome* before he arrived—one of his duller films, in my opinion, although of course I showed it per his request.

I'll give an example of how amusingly outrageous he could be. He loved the films of Alejandro Jodorowsky, and at one point he complained that Jodorowsky's producer wasn't properly distributing them. He was furious about that, he said, so he and his friends had put a curse on the producer. The class thought he was joking and laughed. But then he said the curse was working—the producer had stomach cancer! And the class didn't know whether to laugh or frown or just be aghast! Kenneth was quite the character. Being a bad boy was part of his persona, but each time we talked I found him to be very nice in his own odd way. Incidentally, one of the biggest messages he wanted to get across to my Columbia class was the evil of "the nicotine habit," as he called it. Surprising that the artist who made *Invocation of My Demon Brother* and *Lucifer Rising* and wrote *Hollywood Babylon* felt that one of his missions was to crusade against smoking!

TV, RADIO, AND EDITORS

When did you start making a lot of television appearances?

The first I can remember was on the Boston station WGBH back around 1970. But my first major network appearance was on the *CBS Morning News*, where I talked about new releases with Molly Haskell and Michael Sragow, both of whom I got to know much better in later years.

One of the more interesting shows I did was *Nightline* with Ted Koppel, a major ABC show where the topic was Martin Scorsese's brand-new movie *The Last Temptation of Christ*. The movie hadn't opened yet, but I had seen an almost-final version submitted to the New York Film Festival when I was on the selection committee. I was on the show with Marty in the studio, and through a video hookup we talked with the Rev. Donald Wildmon of the American Family Association in Tupelo, Mississippi, who did not approve of *The Last Temptation of Christ*, although of course he hadn't seen it. I learned later that Marty was distressed when I said I didn't think it was one of his best films—I still don't, by the way—but he and I defended it over the objections of the Mississippi reverend.

The next day I got a call from the editor of the *Monitor*, who was furious because the paper had gotten phone calls protesting that I had defended this obviously profane movie on television. I found out later that it was just a handful of calls, not some sort of mass protest, but my editor was very upset about the whole thing and was talking about firing me. I managed to weather the storm, but I had to cooperate about nixing an ad that was running in *The New York Times*, crediting me as the *Monitor* film critic and quoting me from the *Nightline* show, where I said I hoped people would see the movie and make up their own minds. The *Monitor* complained to Universal Pictures about the ad, and Universal took my name out of it, thus ending the crisis. At a party not long afterward I ran into Jim Jacks, a producer at Universal, and he told me I had been a "very controversial" figure there for a day or two. But things blew over and I kept my job. A curious aspect of this is that Scorsese, who was a seriously religious person, made the film from a sincerely religious point of view, and most of the controversy about it came from Christian fundamentalists and evangelicals, whose religious ideas are quite different from the Christian Science angle and didn't usually bother the *Monitor* very much. So I was a little surprised that the paper raised the roof about this.

In the latter part of the 1980s the Christian Science Publishing Society, or CSPS, started its own radio and television activities, which I was heavily involved in. First they started Monitor Radio, which had me do regular broadcasts for a show called *Monitor Radio*, for another called *World Service*, and for their outlet on Radio Luxembourg in Europe, which had a huge listenership. I did reviews and interviews for these various shows, usually doing retreads of things I had written about for the paper. Among the people I interviewed for radio were the Soviet poet Yevgeny Yevtushenko, the Australian director Fred Schepisi, the Hollywood star Frank Langella, and many others. To avoid constant trips to the Boston studio I did some of the recording at home, and then Monitor Radio hooked up with a radio engineer named Danny Lehrecke, who became a good friend of mine. At first he had a homemade studio in midtown Manhattan, and then he relocated to a building on Nassau Street in lower Manhattan, very close to my own apartment, which was extremely convenient. I also did a lot of recording at the WNYC studio in the Municipal Building, also a short walk from where I lived.

What stood out for me at WNYC was the astonishing frequency of technical glitches—time after time they lost the connection with Boston, or had problems getting sound, et cetera, et cetera. An example of this was one of my interviews with the great director Miloš Forman, which I set up for the *Monitor* and then invited National Public Radio to record as well, since I was also the film critic for NPR's flagship show *All Things Considered*. We set up the interview in the hotel where Miloš was staying, and NPR sent their New York sound engineer, a young woman I liked and worked with regularly, usually in NPR's midtown studio. For some reason it took ages for her to set the equipment properly, get the microphone angles right, and so forth, and Miloš leaned toward me and said he could arrange a whole shooting setup in less time! And when NPR heard the recording afterward, they said I sounded a little "off mic." They used the interview anyway, if memory serves, but those problems have stayed in my mind. Such were the excitements of public-radio technology in the late twentieth century.

Once the CSPS had gotten its radio programming up and running, they started a big television operation as well. It began with a show called *World Monitor*, which ran on the Discovery Channel, and I did numerous segments for that, including interviews with Spike Lee and Susan Seidelman and with the choreographer Paul Taylor, a major favorite of mine. Then the CSPS started the Monitor Channel, its own TV platform. The shows were broadcast from Boston, and the goal was to evolve into a super-channel available by satellite around the world. I appeared regularly on a couple of shows—one was called *Today's Monitor* and the other was *1 Norway Street*, named after the *Monitor*'s address.

I flew up to Boston every other week to tape various things for these programs, and sometimes an additional special as well. This kept me pretty busy, but I got paid for all of it, so I was pleased with the arrangement.

The financial model for these operations didn't prove to be sustainable, though. The TV operation ran from about 1989 to about 1992, and then the whole thing fell apart. They were losing piles of money, and the *Boston Globe* did a lot of reporting on that, which didn't help. So the church abruptly shut the whole thing down—first the TV operation, then the radio operation. They also shut down *World Monitor*, a recently launched monthly magazine that I wrote for a bit. Not too long after this I got an interesting phone call from the managing editor of the *Monitor*, who had seen and enjoyed *sex, lies, and videotape* and wanted to know if Steven Soderbergh had made other movies. We got to talking about the recently shut-down media activities, and he said, "Well, they thought they were following the divine plan and all that, but it just wasn't normal business!" By which he meant that they had expectations about when they would start breaking even and then become profitable, but the projections were wildly off base, and divine intervention hadn't saved the day. For me, it was fun while it lasted, and I was momentarily famous enough in Boston to get recognized on the street once or twice.

The operation posed some challenges for the church, because when they weren't showing their own programs they filled time with material from other television sources, which wasn't always the kind of thing the church would endorse. But it was the financial problem that doomed the enterprise. According to *The New York Times*, in 1992 the church acknowledged losing more than $325 million on the nonprint media activities. A lot of that money had been taken from the newspaper's operating budget, and at one point the editor and other top management resigned in protest. I knew all of them, and I well remember what a dramatic move that was, but it didn't change anything. The media kept rolling along and losing money until the whole thing was shuttered.

There was also another wrinkle that drew a good deal of attention at the time. As I understand it from various accounts, while the CSPS and the church were spending and losing a large fortune on the media operations, a small fortune happened to be available to them from an unusual source. An old-line Christian Scientist with the marvelous name of Bliss Knapp had written a book in the late 1940s about Mary Baker Eddy, the founder of the religion. Knapp had wanted the CSPS to publish it with their imprimatur, but they demurred because the book claimed that Eddy was the human embodiment of a figure in the Book of Revelation—"a woman clothed with the sun, and the moon under her feet"—whereas Eddy tended to present herself as a regular mortal, albeit a spectacularly enlightened one, spiritually speaking. To prod the church and the CSPS into changing their minds, Knapp and a couple of relatives made a bequest of something like $100 million to the church, to be paid on the condition that they publish his book by 1993. The deadline was approaching! Would the honchos of Christian Science forego all that cash, or seize it by publishing a book that might reasonably be deemed heretical? The church arrived at a solution that was either ingenious or desperate, depending on one's point of view. It published Knapp's book along with five other biographies of Eddy, presenting them as a healthy variety of perspectives, and justifying the inclusion of Knapp's volume as a unique contribution by a writer who had known and worked with Eddy personally. Even then, the church got its hands on only about half of the Knapp money, with the other 47 percent going to Stanford University and the Los Angeles County Museum of Art, institutions that were also named in the will and successfully challenged the church's claim to the entire bequest. Quite a saga!

Did the Monitor *have the funding it needed to support its writers when all that money was going to broadcast activities?*

There were cutbacks during that time, but cutbacks weren't rare in any case. Over the years the newspaper oscillated between two basic modes where spending was concerned. In one mode, the idea was to spend whatever was needed— or rather, whatever the paper could reasonably afford—to attract readers with first-rate articles presented in a lively way. In the other mode, we writers were exhorted to tighten our belts, bite our bullets, and economize as much as possible. In the first, relatively openhanded mode, I could fly to Michigan to review an opera. In the second, relatively tightfisted mode, we all had to cut down on big things like travel and small things like subscriptions to other publications. During a belt-tightening period when I was still working in the Boston newsroom, the editors decided we could get more readers for the New England edition if we carried local TV listings, so we writers had to spend time cutting pages out of *TV Guide* and putting them into the *Monitor* format. Fortunately, that didn't last very long.

A redesign of the paper was another tactic the *Monitor* editors sometimes tried to increase its appeal. It never worked, at least not very well. The most drastic change happened when the format changed from broadsheet to tabloid, or "compact," as they euphemistically called the new configuration. I suppose it lowered the cost of printing, but I think it reduced the paper's dignity a bit. A redesign under Kay Fanning's editorship was touted as a terrific step forward and turned out to be just the opposite.

One change involved the Movie Guide, a weekly block of capsule reviews; it's supposed to be a clip-and-save feature, easy to access at a glance, but the new design spread it over three different pages, which is not exactly convenient. Another change that Kay really loved was to continue front-page stories on the back page, so readers didn't have to "hunt around" for the rest of an article they'd started. One problem was that the back page didn't have enough room for all the "jumps," so readers still had to hunt around for things "buried" inside the paper. Another problem was that the back page is a ready-made display space, visible to onlookers when someone else is reading the paper, and when someone puts the paper down with the back side up. Before this change, the back page had the editorial cartoon and the editorials, important and potentially eye-catching material. But now all you saw were the last parts of articles, not eye-catching in the least. I'd always noticed that my young kids regularly glanced at the cartoon when they happened to see the paper on a table, but now it was "buried" inside. A foolish alteration, in my view. Maybe editing is too important to leave to editors.

You've also appeared in many media outlets beyond the Monitor's *operations.*

Yes indeed. I was the film critic for *All Things Considered* on National Public Radio in the late '70s and early '80s, and I appeared on many shows on CNN, CNBC, the Fox News Channel, and so on, mostly in the United States, sometimes in other countries. Fox is obviously a right-wing outfit that I didn't much like—still don't—but we were talking about movies and it was always benign. I appeared a number of times on Bill O'Reilly's show, *The O'Reilly Factor*, and we'd have little disagreements and sometimes it was fun. Catherine Crier had me on her Fox and Court TV shows many times, and I appeared quite a bit on *Countdown with Keith Olbermann* on MSNBC. I was on the old *Hannity and Colmes* show with Sean Hannity, who's still a big deal in cable TV, and Charlie Rose, Joe Scarborough, and Geraldo Rivera have had me as a guest on their shows. And plenty more. Whatever else these things were, they were easier than writing!

Monitor editors

Newspaper writers work with various editors. What were the Monitor *editors like?*

They were a heterogeneous bunch, apart from being Christian Scientists, which was pretty much required for those positions. When I became a full-time critic, the editor of the paper was DeWitt John, the features editor was John Beaufort, and the arts-and-entertainment editor was Harold Rogers, all nice guys whom I got to know fairly well. Hal had been a music critic and John was a former foreign correspondent who later became the theater critic. We got along well, although I gave them a lot of trouble about the fields I was covering. They made me a critic with the understanding that my main field would be music, meaning classical music, but things shifted for some reason, and I ended up writing about various other areas as well. That was okay with me, but I resented not having a field to myself, and I groused so much that I'm a little surprised they didn't just kick me out after a while. In retrospect, I think they were remarkably patient with me.

After a while Hal retired from the paper and Roderick Nordell, the assistant features editor, became the arts-and-entertainment editor. Rod was very intelligent, knowledgeable, conscientious, and pleasant. He was also tied up in psychological knots, scrutinizing every paragraph, every sentence, every word for any possible way it could be interpreted or misinterpreted to mean something that wouldn't be ideal *Monitor* parlance. I once read about a device that could detect nuances of human speech so minute that the human ear couldn't detect them, which raises the question of how the device could possibly be useful. The hypervigilant Rod reminded me of that gizmo.

I could give a jillion examples, but a few should suffice. According to Christian Science, death is a false human belief, so the *Monitor* tended to use words like "death" and "dead" and "die" somewhat sparingly; there's an apocryphal tale that in World War I, reporting in the *Monitor* referred to a battlefield littered with "passed-on mules," and while that's apparently a myth, in a movie review Rod would change "dead body" to "corpse," which sounded a little softer to his ears. He didn't want an artist to be called a "creator," since the only true Creator is God, and like many editors, he also had personal bugaboos—always "child" or "children," for instance, never "kid' or "kids." And more broadly, the more sex, violence, or vulgar language were in a film, the more reader warnings had to be in the review and the fewer column inches Rod would allow it to have. There were many, many of these taboos, and they drove all the critics crazy, not just me. Rod eventually realized the tensions caused by all this, and he left the arts pages to become an editorial writer, which came as a great relief to us writers, and probably to him. I have to add that Rod became a friend as well as an associate, and he was a lovely guy in many ways. Later he became the features editor, returning to my journalistic sphere, but in that position he was a step removed from my daily activities, and by then he had probably mellowed a bit.

The next arts editor was challenging in a new set of ways. I'll call him Alan, no need to give his last name. He had been a critic in New York, and there were signs that he wouldn't be a first-rate editor, or even a third-rate one, since his writing was invariably crammed with misspelled names. Rod had been forced to cook up a special system whereby Alan was required to put a number in brackets [1] after every name to verify that he'd double checked it before sending it in, the sort of discipline you might require for a recalcitrant middle-schooler.

The inauspicious auguries proved true when he arrived in the Boston newsroom as an editor. On one of his first days he vetoed my use of the phrase "stopped the conversation dead," not because it's a cliché (which it is, I admit) but because it had the word "dead" in it. Not even Rod would have been that picky. But it soon turned out that Alan was fairly easy-going about such things, not because he thought carefully and reached considered opinions, but because his mind and memory were extraordinarily disordered, and he simply wasn't able to police the verbal territory in consistent ways. As for organizing tasks and working with the newsroom team, he was a disaster. He forgot almost everything he was told, unless he was told by an editor above him in the chain, in which case he would remember forever and act on it long after its relevance had vanished. I used to say he had a mind exactly like a sieve—most things flowed out of it within seconds, but when something got stuck there, it was impossible to dislodge. He was a very pleasant and nice-looking guy—his wife had once been a finalist in one of the biggest American beauty pageants—but as a journalist he was terrible.

Here's an example. In my review of the biopic *Raging Bull*, I wrote that the story covered many events in Jake LaMotta's life, from the heights of winning the middleweight championship to the depths of throwing a fight. Alan evidently feared we'd get in trouble for saying LaMotta had thrown a fight, even though LaMotta publicly admitted it and everyone who read sports pages knew all about it. So he changed my review to say the movie shows LaMotta "allegedly throwing a fight deliberately," adding the ridiculous "allegedly" and the equally ridiculous redundancy of "throwing a fight deliberately." How else could one throw a fight? Such was the craziness possible at one of the world's allegedly great newspapers.

One more example. I've talked with the very good actor Cliff Robertson more than once, and we had a very good interview in 1980, when he directed and starred in a movie called *The Pilot*, about an airline pilot with a drinking problem. Cliff himself was an active flyer who loved planes, and this was his effort to call attention to a real social problem. Alan called me about something or other and mentioned that the Robertson interview would be in the next day's paper. I said I was glad to write that article, since the movie dealt with such an important topic. Alan asked me what the topic was—he either hadn't read the article or had already forgotten what it was about—and I said it spotlighted the problem of drinking by airline pilots. Alan went into a panic, bleating "What?!" and yelping that he had to get it off the page before the paper was finalized for the day. I tried to calm him down—the *Monitor* loved material that put alcohol in a bad light—but he instantly hung up. Calling me back a little later, he told me with great relief that he'd managed to pull the article out and replace it with something else. I asked him why, and he answered that he'd used a photo of Cliff with a smile on his face—hence his panic when I told him what the movie was about. I said he should run the article with a different photo, and he agreed. Then weeks went by, because he had probably forgotten about it. When it finally ran, the movie was no longer playing, so we were way behind the curve. But there was my interview, with the same smiley-face photo that had caused the panic!

This wasn't the only time Alan acted foolishly, and everyone who worked with him was aware of his ineptitude, except the editors who could have removed him. When one of those editors finally saw the light and Alan returned to writing instead of editing, I asked why he had managed to hold on so long, and even to become an editor in the first place. The editor answered that Alan was the kind of person who was always good in the audition, always bad in the performance. That sums it up nicely.

Other editors did screwy things as well. When I wrote that the comedy in a new movie came in small doses, for instance, an editor wouldn't allow "doses" because it sounded medical. And in the 1980s there was an arts editor so inexperienced that they gave her the title "coordinator" rather than "editor," although she referred to herself as "editor" from the get-go. Her name was Kathy, and like Alan, she was ridiculously submissive to what she thought the higher editors wanted. I got into a tussle with the top editor, Kay Fanning, when she abruptly decided we wouldn't review horror movies anymore. Not even negative reviews, I asked? That's right, not even those. Not even when a horror movie breaks the mold by being humane and optimistic, I asked? That's right, not even then. Not even when every other publication, and movie fans around the world, are buzzing about a film, I asked? That's right, we'll just ignore it. Of course, the *Monitor* was owned and operated by a fairly conservative church, but it had been ever thus, and the paper had reviewed horror movies without incident for decades. But this was now the policy, and Kathy's grim enforcement brought the absurdity of the situation to the surface. In the middle '80s a science-fiction comedy called *Morons from Outer Space* arrived on the screen, and I filed a little capsule review, and Kathy phoned me in a rage to ask why I had broken the rules by reviewing a horror movie!

I should also say something about the issue of potentially offensive content in movies. In my early years as a critic the landscape changed drastically—until the middle 1960s you rarely heard even a "damn" or "hell" in mainstream films, nudity was mostly forbidden, and violence was kept within bounds. But the later '60s opened the door to nudity, increasingly explicit sex, increasingly graphic violence, and every vulgarism there is, and although the MPAA rating system arrived in late 1968, many years passed before ads explained *why* a movie was rated G or R or whatever. Since some moviegoers are very irked by the excesses of "adult" content, the *Monitor*'s policy was to weave a warning about vulgar words, sex, nudity, and violence into our reviews. This seemed reasonable to me, although I tried to soft-pedal my warnings in keeping with my own liberal-minded attitudes. Everything proceeded smoothly until someone in the church administration—which hardly ever interfered with the paper's day-to-day activities—complained about an insufficient warning in some review and ordered that warnings about offensive content must be placed in a special box, highlighted with boldface type, and placed near the top of any review where a warning might be useful. In practice, this visual emphasis gave the impression that a note about nudity or language—this film contains a few four-letter words or brief partial nudity—was the most important thing we had to say about the picture. Even the paper's top editors saw how absurd this was, and the managing editor came up with a workaround. The person who mandated this said it didn't have to be applied to columnists, so I became a "columnist," my reviews were labeled "columns," and we could revert to our normal practice. Problem solved. And what a silly problem it was.

Since that time, the MPAA has specified the reasons for giving a particular rating to a film, and it's become common practice for newspapers to include a note about potentially problematic content. A good idea, I think. I'll add that I've occasionally been invited to speak or appear on a panel at the one and only Christian Science institution of higher education, Principia College in Illinois, and I once came equipped with video clips containing a great deal of four-letter language. I asked the college president whether it would be all right to show them, and he said sure, that wasn't a hang-up on the campus. So the college was more permissive than the paper, for whatever that's worth.

It's worth mentioning that movies weren't the only contentious artform at the paper, and some editors had reactionary cultural views. There was a top editor who disliked modern art, for instance, so getting a picture of a modernist painting into the paper could be tricky. As for serious music, I did an interview with the titanic composer John Cage, regarded by many as the most influential composer of the twentieth century. A terrific piece for us to have, but the managing editor made it drastically shorter—he didn't approve of Cage's theories, it turned out, and he wasn't going to give the hugely important composer more than a few inches of our valuable space. Preposterous. I'll also mention a disagreement that came up when I reviewed a movie adaptation of Shakespeare's *Julius Caesar*. It was a bad movie, and Jason Robards was so terrible as Brutus that I said he sounded like a student reading the lines for the first time. The editor said I was being too harsh and drastically softened what I'd written. A few years later I interviewed Robards over lunch, and I diplomatically asked him about that film. He said the production was such a disaster that he decided to just say the lines as quickly as possible and get away from it. So I'd been right! Nice to have that vindication, not that it made any difference to anyone except me.

On a slightly different topic, it's a truism among movie critics that it's almost always awful if your editor is a movie buff. Movie buffs take various forms, from trivia enthusiasts to thoughtful viewers, but while a given movie buff may or may not have a solid understanding of film, it would be a very rare specimen who had the everyday immersion in the medium that a professional critic has. Near the end of my time at the *Monitor* the managing editor was a movie buff who combined a know-it-all attitude with a sense of moral superiority that was really obnoxious. We clashed quite a lot, and although I survived the skirmishes once again, there were harrowing moments along the way.

All this must have been frustrating for you.

Hearing how things like this shook down at the *Monitor*, a person might reasonably ask why I stayed at a paper where such goofiness went on. So I hasten to say that while things like this happened more often than they should have, they were not typical occurrences. The paper mostly operated in a lucid and competent manner. Editors like Alan and Kathy were the exception, not the rule, and the worst of them (the anomalous Alan aside) didn't last long in the job. I'll also mention an arts editor named Fred, who started his tenure by rewording my warning about some foul language in a movie, making it much longer and blunter than it should have been. I pointed out that almost every movie contained some foul language, and if we used heavy-handed warnings like this routinely, our film coverage would look petty and backward. He got the message, and soon turned into one of the best arts editors I ever had, trusting me and the other writers to handle things according to our own experience and expertise. So all in all, the *Monitor* was a good place to work. And most publications, if not all publications, have their share of quirks, eccentricities, and employees who aren't up to the job.

I think one key to my longevity at the paper—almost forty years, and I survived more than one large-scale layoff caused by budget cuts—was the fact that due to my Christian Science family background, I knew the lingo and had a good sense of how the editors tended to think. A good example is an article I wrote about Alan Arkin after I interviewed him. I felt he had grown a lot as an actor over his career up to that time, and I also remembered him as a member of the Tarriers, a commercial folk-singing group in the '50s. I asked him about his success at different kinds of performing, and he said he'd never believed in limiting himself, which happens to be a phrase I'd heard a number of times—"Don't limit yourself!"—from the religious folks I knew as a kid. So I used that quote in the lead of my article, and the editors promptly placed the piece on the front page. I'd like to think it got the spotlight because of its overall excellence, but I strongly suspect the editors just loved that opening quote.

Were you ever tempted to be an editor at the Monitor?

Far from being tempted, I had to fend it off. At one point the editor of the paper, Kay Fanning, decided I should be the arts editor. I accepted the offer and told the other writers in the arts department, who were delighted, partly because it meant Alan wouldn't be in the mix anymore. But very soon I realized what a mistake this would be. It would mean moving back to Boston, a city I didn't love as much as New York, and more important, it would mean sticking to all the *Monitor* rules, not being edgy and pushing the envelope, which I saw as my true calling. So I called them and said I'd changed my mind, I wouldn't take the position. And they wouldn't take no for an answer—they sweetened the offer, threw more money into the deal, and pushed me as hard as they could. I didn't budge, though, and eventually they backed off, assuring me the job would still be mine if I ever wanted it. The episode was flattering, but I've never regretted turning the offer down.

Was the Monitor *an influential publication? Was it widely read when you were there, and did your writing have real effects on film and culture?*

Well, hey, we weren't *The New York Times* or *The Washington Post*. The paper's circulation wasn't high—somewhere around 200,000 when I started there in the 1960s and probably less than half of that when I took early retirement in 2005. But its reputation has always been high. It's won a number of Pulitzer Prizes, and when I started it was said to be one of President Lyndon Johnson's favorite papers. And in the '70s they started a syndication service through which other newspapers reprinted *Monitor* content—at its peak there were about 200 newspapers in the system, with a combined total of around 20 million readers. Publicists and press agents took us quite seriously even before the syndication service began, and even more seriously when so many potential readers were in the mix. I'm sure those days are long gone, but people knew about and respected the paper even if they'd never read it or even laid eyes on it.

And every now and then some prominent artistic type would show some personal interest in the paper. The great playwright Horton Foote once told me he got a better sense of the Off-Off-Broadway theater scene from my articles than from the *Village Voice*, and Neil Simon once told me he was about to give up on one of his plays after a terrible out-of-town tryout, but changed his mind and kept working on it—ultimately with a successful outcome—when the review by our regular theater critic clued him in about what the essential problem was. And an amusing thing involving Stanley Kubrick happened just after I became a *Monitor* critic. The review of *2001: A Space Odyssey* was written by one of the senior film critics, but a young second-stringer named John Allen loved the picture so much that he wrote an article about it—the kind of thing called a "think piece" in the trade—and it ran as a two-page centerspread in the paper. John then traipsed over to Kubrick's office in New York, sat there and waited for the maestro to arrive, and showed it to him. Kubrick asked how many people read the paper, and John told him, whereupon Kubrick said the article shouldn't stay hidden in the *Monitor*, and had it reprinted as a full-page ad in *The New York Times*. I doubt if any *Monitor* film review has reached more people, but it wasn't in the *Monitor*'s own pages!

The bottom line is that the *Monitor* was a good berth, but more for the paper's general reputation than for its number of steady readers or its direct influence on film, theater, or music. In terms of my own recognizability, writing for a newspaper or magazine is never the best way to cultivate personal fame. I was recognized on the street during the run of *Monitor* television, and I was recognized on the subway during my time with the New York Film Festival, and during my years as the film critic for NPR's *All Things Considered* I got more audience feedback than usually came my way at the paper. Anyone looking for fame should look elsewhere than print journalism.

ORGANIZATIONS
AND FESTIVALS

Tell about your time as chair of the New York Film Critics Circle.

When I became a full-time film critic, I thought about joining the official film-critic groups, but I decided to wait for them to invite me. One day I found a message on my answering machine from Kathleen Carroll, the *Daily News* critic who was chair of the NYFCC that year, saying I'd just been voted in as a member, so I never had to apply at all. The group's only real activity was (and is) to vote on awards at the end of the year and present them at a banquet a few weeks later. I used to joke that the biggest challenge of being in the NYFCC was remembering that you were *in* the NYFCC during all the other months.

I hadn't been in the group very long before a recent chair, Bruce Williamson of *Playboy*, asked if I'd like to run the show. I should mention that I was quite close to Bruce, and I found it amusing that the *Playboy* and *Christian Science Monitor* critics were so tight. For some reason I wasn't at the meeting when that vote took place, but things went as planned, and I became vice-chair for that year—the chair was Joseph Gelmis, the longtime *Newsday* critic—and then became chair. My first responsibility was to preside over the awards voting, which happened in a room at the News-paper Guild—we sat around a long table, so we were really an oval rather than a circle—and then I set about the main tasks: notifying the winners and asking them to attend the banquet, usually through their publicists or the publicists for the movies they'd won for, and then recruiting a second set of celebrities to present the awards at the ceremony. I had a lot of help from Bruce and also Judith Crist, a famous critic who'd been with *The New York Herald-Tribune* and many other outlets and became a very good personal friend.

The awards were for movies of 1987, and the picture that swept many categories was *Broadcast News*, which won the prize for best film. Jack Nicholson was named best actor for that picture—and also for *Ironweed* and *The Witches of Eastwick*, all released that year—and at the ceremony I was struck by how positively delighted he was to get our award. Holly Hunter, the winner for best actress, and James L. Brooks, the winner for best director and best screen-play, also came from *Broadcast News*. Vittorio Storaro was named best cinematographer for *The Last Emperor*, Morgan Freeman won best supporting actor for *Street Smart*—that one was orchestrated by Pauline Kael, notorious for her network of critical cronies—and Vanessa Redgrave won best supporting actress for *Prick Up Your Ears*. The best foreign-language picture was Lasse Hallström's dramedy *My Life as a Dog*.

As always, the awards ceremony was held at Sardi's, which at that time was still a legendary venue in the Broadway theater district. And the evening went well. My sons, then in their middle teens, checked in the illustrious arrivals, which wasn't all that easy because (oops) no one had put the guest list in alphabetical order. Most of the winners were present, and although Storaro couldn't be there, I invited the equally magnificent Sven Nykvist to accept the prize for him. Holly Hunter also sent word that she couldn't attend. Fairly or unfairly, she was said to be so disliked in the film community that we had a hard time finding someone to stand in for her. Daniel Day-Lewis, who admired Redgrave with a passion, agreed to come to New York and present her award so he could meet her in person, but at the last minute she had visa trouble—her political activism rubbed American authorities the wrong way—so poor Daniel was out of luck, although he showed up anyway and took the let-down with good grace.

We had a number of great presenters—Wallace Shawn was a favorite—but the biggest challenge was finding a broadcast-news bigwig to present the *Broadcast News* award. The movie is a fairly biting satire of the TV-news business, and that scared off every TV personality we approached, until the biggest bigwig of them all, Walter Cronkite, said he'd be delighted to do it. He was as genial and charismatic as anyone could wish, and he spoke glowingly about the film, calling it "a whale of a good movie." It was a terrific climax to the evening. I'll add that Cronkite was far and away the biggest non-movie celebrity we had at the event, and I hoped that the chance to meet him would help compensate Daniel Day-Lewis for missing out on Vanessa Redgrave, but then I realized that Daniel was from England and had hardly even heard of the legendary TV journalist! Again, though, he was gracious about his disappointment.

Was your second term as chair similar to the first?

My second term started with a year as vice-chair for Owen Gleiberman, the estimable *Entertainment Weekly* critic. Then came my own stint as chair. Per our usual schedule, we presented the awards for 2000 at a banquet in January 2001, and we had moved from Sardi's to Windows on the World, the posh restaurant atop the World Trade Center, a three-minute walk from my apartment. The group could afford the steep price of Windows on the World because someone had hit on the brilliant idea of having a printed program for the evening, replete with ads paid for by our publications and the movie companies whose pictures were being honored. Our best picture prize went to Steven Soderbergh's *Traffic*, and Steven was named best director for that picture and also for *Erin Brockovich*. Tom Hanks won best actor for his marathon performance in *Cast Away* and Kenneth Lonergan's *You Can Count on Me* produced two winners, Kenny for best screenplay and Laura Linney for best actress. Benicio del Toro was voted best supporting actor for *Traffic* and Marcia Gay Harden was best supporting actress for *Pollock*, the Jackson Pollock biopic. Other awards went to Peter Pau for the cinematography of *Crouching Tiger, Hidden Dragon* and to Edward Yang's *Yi Yi (A One and a Two)* for best foreign-language film. Peter Lord and Nick Park's *Chicken Run* won for best animated film, and David Gordon Green's *George Washington* was voted best first film. Best non-fiction film went to Aviva Kempner's *The Life and Times of Hank Greenberg*, about the celebrated Jewish baseball player, and although Aviva is an old friend, I cringe when I remember how annoyed everyone was when her acceptance speech went on and on and on and on; a little later Matthew Broderick presented an award and poked fun at her by starting with something like, "I was born in a log cabin…" We also gave special awards to the Shooting Gallery, a New York production company that folded a few months afterward, and to Rialto Pictures for reissuing Jules Dassin's 1955 classic *Rififi*.

Our roster of presenters was spectacular. Conan O'Brien presented the best picture award, and others there included Richard Gere, Mike Nichols, Paul Schrader, Ellen Burstyn, et cetera, et cetera. Several months later the attacks of 9/11 decimated the World Trade Center, destroying Windows on the World and cutting short what might have been a long-lasting NYFCC affiliation with the restaurant, which was an ideal showcase for our event. When we close a joint, I remarked after 9/11, we really close it.

I remember that you lived very near Ground Zero.

My apartment at 176 Broadway was about a two-minute walk from the twin towers of the World Trade Center, so yep, I was a Ground Zero resident. As it happened, I was away at the Toronto film festival when the attacks occurred, but my then-wife was home, and my son Jeremy and his wife lived just as close to the towers, so I was in high anxiety until I learned everyone was okay. When the immediate panic was over, they walked over the Brooklyn Bridge to my son Craig's apartment in Brooklyn and all was well. My building was evacuated for a couple of weeks. Jeremy and Tanya's building was evacuated for a couple of years!

Returning to our main topic, you also chaired the National Society of Film Critics.

Yes, for a decade. I was asked to take the post by Peter Rainer, who was chair before me, and Elisabeth Weis, the executive director. Both are good friends of mine, and I was glad to say yes, whereupon the group voted its approval. The National Society comes closest to being a real meritocracy, for what that's worth, because most critics organizations have a geographical orientation. To join the NYFCC you have to submit writing samples so the members can decide if you're good enough, but you also have to work in New York, or write for a New York-based publication, or in my case, work from the New York bureau of a national paper. Members of the National Society come from across the country, and the only criterion for membership is first-rate writing.

The NSFC bestows annual awards, like the NYFCC and other such outfits, and at the time I joined, the members could vote in more than one way—in person at a meeting in the Algonquin Hotel or by a ballot mailed in advance; nowadays there's still a New York meeting, in a room at the Film Society of Lincoln Center, as well as a West Coast meeting with a Zoom hookup to the New York conclave, and members are also free to vote by internet from wherever they want. There's no ceremony or banquet, though— we just mail fancy-looking certificates to the winners. The distinguishing characteristic of the National Society is that every ballot is read aloud as it's counted, so everyone knows how everyone else has voted. This takes time, and typical voting sessions go on for hours; fortunately, there's a business meeting on the previous day, so housekeeping matters are out of the way when the voting starts. When I was chair, I missed one meeting because I was serving on the international critics' jury at the Palm Springs Film Festival, and wouldn't you know, every award was decided on the first ballot! Probably the only time that ever happened, and I wasn't there to enjoy it.

Membership lapses in most critic groups if you move to a different area or stop working as a regular critic, but once you're accepted into the National Society you're in it for good, although you go into "inactive" status if you stop seeing enough films to cast informed ballots. I've been a member of other groups, including the Online Film Critics

Society, which made me a "special honorary member" when I took early retirement from the *Monitor* in 2005. And I've belonged to the International Federation of Film Critics, known by its European acronym FIPRESCI, for many years, and have sat on FIPRESC juries at various film festivals. The best thing a critics group can do is call attention to movies that would otherwise be overlooked or undervalued. Most of the awards go to prominent and well-publicized pictures, but I'm always pleased when we honor an under-recognized gem.

Film festivals have been a major part of your activities. Which were the first ones you attended?

The first two were the Cannes festival in 1974 and the Los Angeles Film Exposition, known as Filmex, in 1975. Going off to Cannes in 1974 was a major event for me because it was the first major film festival I attended. I didn't have any particular agenda for films I wanted to see—it was such a huge, bustling festival that there was plenty to choose from. The first film I saw was the opening-night feature, Fellini's *Amarcord*, which was being screened out of competition. I was somewhat jetlagged, so when I found myself disappointed with the movie, I felt that maybe the problem lay in my fatigue rather than the movie itself. Then again, I do think Fellini's career declined after *8½* and *Juliet of the Spirits*, so maybe I wasn't entirely off base.

Looking back at the Cannes program that year, I can't always remember whether my first viewing of a movie was there or later on back home, but some pretty distinguished films were on view. Among them were Fassbinder's *Ali: Fear Eats the Soul*, Ken Russell's *Mahler*, *The Last Detail* by Hal Ashby, *My Cousin Angelica* by Carlos Saura, Pasolini's *Arabian Nights*, which I'm not so fond of, and *The Conversation* by Coppola, which won the festival's top prize. I also remember *The Holy Office* by the great Mexican director Arturo Ripstein, whom I interviewed some years later at the San Francisco festival, and *A Bigger Splash* by Jack Hazan, starring the painter David Hockney as himself. Others included Resnais's *Stavisky…*, Spielberg's *The Sugarland Express*, Altman's *Thieves Like Us*, Dušan Makavejev's *Sweet Movie*, and Jacques Tati's *Parade*, the weakest film by that great director. I'll also mention a less famous film, *Les Violons du bal* by Michel Drach, whom I got to know a little back in New York.

I thought it would be fun to interview a member of the Cannes jury, so I talked with Irwin Shaw, the only American on the panel that year. I later learned how the jury works. It's isolated from the public and also from the thousands of journalists at the festival, so its prizes are sometimes surprising and occasionally inscrutable, although that year *The Conversation* was a splendid Palme d'or winner. Another quirk of the festival is that the films shown on the opening and closing nights tend to be chosen more for splashiness than for quality; the closing feature in 1974 was Irvin Kershner's comedy *S*P*I*E*S*, an awful *M*A*S*H* knockoff that has been deservedly forgotten.

The following year I went to Filmex, where one of the events was a tribute to Irene Dunne, featuring clips from any number of her movies. The festival was very proud of screening all those clips from full 35mm prints, an incredibly cumbersome process that stretched the tribute into an hours-long marathon that definitely outlived its welcome, at least for me. It was hosted by Roddy McDowall, and I had a pleasant talk with him even though I was told he didn't do many interviews. I interviewed Buck Henry as well, a very important screenwriter and occasional actor, and my impression of him was that he was highly intelligent, discussing Sigmund Freud and psychoanalytic theory at one point. I also met the festival proprietors, Gary Essert and Gary Abrahams, called the two Garys by one and all. Nice guys.

In the next few years I didn't do much festival-going, since there was plenty to do in New York, and I wanted to limit my traveling when my kids were young. I did participate in various junkets, as we've discussed, and I certainly traveled when there was a good reason. As mentioned, for instance, in 1982 I flew to the University of Michigan School of Music to see Altman's production of Stravinsky's opera *The Rake's Progress*. I took my son Jeremy along—he and Craig were eleven—since he was the violinist of the family. I got deeply involved in the film-festival world in the '80s when I was invited to join the New York Film Festival selection committee.

The New York Film Festival

How did you come to serve on the New York Film Festival selection committee?

Therein lies an interesting tale. The parent organization of the NYFF is the Film Society of Lincoln Center, and at that time—the middle to late 1980s—its main activities were presenting the festival, co-sponsoring the annual New

Directors/New Films series with the Museum of Modern Art, publishing *Film Comment* magazine, and putting on an annual gala, designed to raise funds by showcasing a Hollywood star or auteur who gets to bask in adulation for a few hours. I attended the galas for Alfred Hitchcock, Bette Davis, Barbara Stanwyck, Woody Allen, Paul Newman and George Cukor, to name ones I particularly remember.

The festival was started in 1963 by Richard Roud and Amos Vogel, who wanted to encourage the recognition of cinema as a serious artform. In keeping with that aim, the festival was highly selective in its programming and didn't give awards, since getting selected for the festival was a prize in itself. Films were chosen by a five-member selection committee with two permanent members who worked for the society and three rotating members, usually well-known movie critics, who served three-year terms. Roud chaired the committee from the late '60s through 1987. But by the middle '80s there was a growing sense that the festival needed a fresh perspective, broadening its horizons and reducing its strong emphasis on Western European art pictures. One person who felt that way was a person who mattered: Joanne Koch, the society's executive director. She decided to engineer a coup, ousting Roud and bringing in a new programming director with a younger, more expansive outlook. Joanne persuaded the society's board to support her, and the coup succeeded: Roud was out and the much younger Richard Peña, who had been a film programmer in Chicago, was in.

But things were complicated by aggressive news coverage in *The New York Times*, which took the position that ousting Richard R. was an outrage against the New York film community and the cinema itself. Another complication was the state of the selection committee. (I'll use some last-name initials here, because plenty of Richards were involved in all this. More than one David was in the mix as well.) One of the permanent members, Richard R., had been expelled. The other permanent member, *Time* film critic and *Film Comment* editor Richard Corliss, immediately resigned, although he went out of his way to tell me his resignation wasn't a protest but rather a power move designed to get Roud back into position—a power move that clearly didn't have enough power. As for the rotating members, one critic's three-year term was expiring, and David Denby, the *New York* magazine critic, resigned to show his anger at Roud's ouster. That left the *Philadelphia Inquirer* critic Carrie Rickey, who was happy to continue, but for a brief spell the five-member committee had exactly one member.

Joanne went into action, replacing Richard R. and Richard C. with Richard P. and Wendy Keys, a long-time FSLC programmer and administrator. But the road got bumpy when various critics were invited to join the committee and publicly refused, either out of loyalty to Roud or because they believed accusations in the *Times* that Joanne had been trying to strong-arm the committee into accepting movies the committee didn't want. *Village Voice* critic J. Hoberman, *Wall Street Journal* critic Julie Salamon, *Vanity Fair* critic Stephen Schiff, and *New Yorker* critic Terrence Rafferty, all of whom I've known for years, were the nay-sayers, and while Julie said it was the public brouhaha that made her reluctant, Stephen opined that joining the committee under these circumstances would be like accepting "the standard Vichy argument," which he regarded as "the refuge of scoundrels." Yikes! Tempers were flaring, and embarrassment was descending on the Film Society of Lincoln Center.

So call me a scoundrel if you like. I had presided over the New York Film Critics Circle awards at Sardi's in January, and our guests had included Joanne and other FSLC notables, and Joanne invited me to join the committee soon thereafter. Not wanting another public refusal, they got Bruce Williamson to ask me whether I'd be willing to accept, and I saw no reason not to. I knew and liked Richard Roud, but I had no personal loyalty to him, and as someone who'd attended every NYFF event for years, I was well acquainted with the territory. I readily accepted, and Phillip Lopate, a film buff as well as an essayist, joined me and Carrie as members with three-year terms. Things worked out so well that Phillip and I were invited to remain for a fourth year, and I set some kind of record by serving for five consecutive years. Stuart Klawans, the superb critic for *The Nation*, replaced Carrie when her term expired, and *Newsweek* critic David Ansen joined when Phillip departed. Along with Richard P. and Wendy, they became warm personal friends as well as valued colleagues.

How did you go about choosing the festival's programs?

We made our selections per the committee's established routine. In early May we headed for the Cannes Film Festival, subsidized by the NYFF and housed in the Hotel Splendid, an elegant old place just a few minutes' walk from the sprawling Palais des Festivals, where most of the screenings take place. A month or so later we hunkered down in the Preview 9 screening room at 1600 Broadway for two weeks of intensive viewing. We had the screening room to ourselves, and the projectionist, Don Schul, kept the reels spinning with marvelous efficiency. We watched in respectful silence when a movie seemed like a possible keeper, and we stopped them without mercy when a picture clearly wasn't festival material. Very few submissions came to us on video in the '80s, although we'd occasionally watch a cassette in someone's apartment or in the film society's office. That changed over the years, and many pictures were coming via video by the time I left the committee.

Some of the items we watched at 1600 Broadway were movies some or all of us had already seen at Cannes but weren't sure we'd been able to judge properly, since the Cannes screening schedule was hectic and sometimes exhausting. Cannes had major press screenings every morning and evening, and second-tier entries—often way better than the big-deal pictures—were screened without letup in large and small auditoriums in the Palais and else- where. The main slate at Cannes was the Official Competi- tion; the most important sidebar was the program called Un Certain Regard; and also of interest was the Quinzaine des Réalisateurs, or Directors' Fortnight, which has since been renamed. And there was the Marché du Film, where films were screened for potential distributors and exhibitors; for that you needed a special pass, which the NYFF bought for us in years when we deemed it necessary.

For all regular screenings you needed an official Cannes pass, and true to French tradition, the credentials were orga- nized in a rigid hierarchy. For a while I had a white "soirée" pass, which admitted me to everything, including the public evening shows at the vast Grand Auditorium Lumière, where formal dress was required. The first time I went to Cannes, in 1974, I had showed up at a "soirée" screening with a necktie instead of a bowtie, and sure enough, the usher wouldn't let me in. Fortunately, my friend Catherine Verret from the French Film Office was nearby, and she interceded on my behalf, whereupon a guard escorted me to an obscure little room and handed me a cardboard bowtie, which I pinned to my shirt, whereupon I was allowed into the theater. If you were wearing a hand-painted Picasso necktie, it seems, you'd be too lowbrow for evening shows at the Grand Auditorium Lumière, but with a cardboard bowtie you were fully quali- fied to attend. Bizarre, bizarre.

After some years with a white pass I was switched into the pink-pass category, which bestowed the same rights and privileges as the white ones except admission to the "soirée" screenings, which were a pain to attend anyway. But having a little dot on your pink pass was crucial, since without that *pastille* certain things were off limits. I always had the little dot. And I had something far more rare, an *"accompagnant"* pass for my wife, which gave her entry into almost every-thing, far surpassing the holders of sub-pink-*pastille* passes, even though her sole connection with the movie world was being my *accompagnant*. Bizarre again, but good for my domestic arrangements.

After five enjoyable years I exited the committee but kept up yearly attendance at Cannes, and my former NYFF colleagues remained close pals. Now the *Monitor* was paying my way, so I had to give up the lovely room with terrace that Lincoln Center had provided me with hitherto. My good friend Harlan Jacobson, a former *Film Comment* editor who founded and ran the estimable Talk Cinema film series in several American cities, suggested that I get a space in the place where he was staying, which he described as a combination of the Versailles Palace and a college dorm. Exactly right! It was a floor in a vast old chateau not too far from town, rented during the Cannes festival by Jerome Rudes, the founder of the French-American Film Work-shop in Avignon.

Soon after arriving I learned that Jerry sublet every inch of the place to people like me, which was the college-dorm aspect of the experience. And just one bathroom for all of us, complete with a broken light fixture, which meant bringing in a lamp plugged outside the door, which meant the door couldn't completely close. Going to Cannes wasn't all glitz and glamour! Things worked out all right, but Harlan and I rented an apartment of our own for the next few years, quite close to the Palais and perfect for our purposes. Lots of logistics are in play on the festival-going scene. And there was certainly some glitz and glamour, by the way. I was well acquainted with the producer Ed Pressman, for instance, and most years he would host a terrific lunch at the Cap d'An-tibes Hotel, with marvelous food and all sorts of fascinating people. Not only did I have one of my talks with Oliver Stone at one of Ed's luncheons, I had lunch with Oliver's mother!

As for my *Monitor* writing, during the '90s the editors wanted more coverage of people and "fun" at Cannes and less coverage of the film festival's actual films. I did my best to make them happy, lining up interviews and going to press conferences, but still giving top priority to the movies. The paper had always been suspicious of what they called "elite" material, which for some editors was anything that seemed too brainy or offbeat or "foreign," even when "An International Daily Newspaper" was their slogan. But in the '90s and early 2000s they leaned increasingly in the populist direction, and this played a small but significant role in my decision to take early retirement in 2005. That said, some of the "people" coverage was pleasurable for me. I was in a small group that met with Nicole Kidman, a very smart and personable actor. I had a great talk with the eccentric commix writer Harvey Pekar when the movie about him, *American Splendor*, arrived in 2003. I renewed acquaintances with people like Terry Gilliam, Mike Leigh, and Errol Morris at Cannes, and I could give many other examples of pleasant encounters that pleased my editors, or at least didn't displease them.

Moscow, Vienna, Toronto, and beyond

You also attended many other festivals. Were they all interesting and worthwhile?

They generally were. After the '70s the *Monitor* didn't allow traveling on someone else's dime, and the paper's own budget was pretty limited, although they sent me to Cannes every year. But until the 2000s it was okay to attend film festivals at the festival's expense, and some festivals invited me every year. One was the huge and eclectic Toronto festival, which would invite me to provide some service to justify paying my expenses—I introduced a screening, or chaired a "micromeeting" on some film-industry topic, or wrote a front-page column for the festival's daily publication. The World Film Festival in Montreal also brought me back every year, and I visited the Vancouver festival as well. I did onstage talks with Mike Leigh and Stan Brakhage at the Telluride festival in the Colorado mountains, and I served on festival or FIPRESCI juries at various venues.

Jury experiences were mostly good, sometimes less than satisfactory. One of the latter was at the Moscow film festival in 2002. The festival transported us jurors to the festival center in a van full of cigarette smoke, which was a drag; fortunately, I realized it was a fairly short walk to the auditorium from the Hotel Metropole, where I was staying, so I started going there on my own. Then the president of the jury, the veteran French critic Marcel Martin, left town before the screenings were over, so FIPRESCI asked me to take care of the final details, which I hadn't planned on. When we had our final meeting to decide on the best film, the festival sent "observers" to sit in, and they overtly pressured us to choose a Russian picture. I intensely disliked this lobbying, but not everyone on the jury felt the same, and the prize went to a Russian movie, *The Cuckoo* by Aleksandr Rogozhkin, a World War II drama. Although it's a perfectly good picture, the circumstances were discomfiting, and then it took an incredibly long time for everyone to agree on the exact wording of the award. At least we managed to split the prize with *The Supplement* by Krzysztof Zanussi, the great Polish filmmaker.

I should also mention that my pocket was picked on the Moscow subway, and I made the great mistake of reporting this to the police, who put me through a long and point-less session of looking at mugshots and describing the theft while a cop laboriously wrote down every word in long-hand. No one in the police station spoke English, so there's no telling what would have happened if the festival hadn't supplied me with an interpreter. That was a low point of my festival-going career.

Another dubious experience happened at the Palm Springs festival, run by David Ansen, my former NYFF colleague. The festival recruited me for the FIPRESCI jury, and it turned out that dozens of films were in the running. That was fine in itself, but I was the only jury member who took the trouble of actually watching them all, which took ages. Then the other jurors, having shirked some of their duties, insisted on honoring Maren Ade's *Toni Erdmann*, a film I don't much like, and a boring choice anyway, since the film had already gotten awards elsewhere, and my fellow jurors' main argument in its favor was that a woman directed it. Oh well, you can't win them all.

By contrast, I had no complaints about festivals in Vienna, Bermuda, Miami, Newport, Tribeca, the Sarasota French film festival in Florida, the Mill Valley Film Festival in California, and elsewhere. In one of my years at Sundance, the festival flew me to Park City for the express purpose of moderating a dialogue between two all-time-great non-fiction filmmakers, Frederick Wiseman and Werner Herzog, because the festival—and specifically the wonderful Diane Weyerman, who worked with Sundance then—feared that Werner's disdain for cinema-vérité might produce friction with Fred, a pioneer and brilliant practitioner of that form, and thought my moderation would get us over any rough spots. I already knew both filmmakers, and with no effort on my part we dispensed with any potential conflict in the first couple of minutes—everyone agreed that labels aren't important and what counts is the quality of the cinema. No friction at all! And speaking of Werner, in one of my visits to the San Francisco festival I did an onstage interview with him at the enormous old Castro Theatre before a sold-out audience of Herzog admirers. Our talk was followed by a screening of his latest film, *The Wild Blue Yonder*, and people were streaming out of the auditorium soon after it started. Our conversation was more popular than the picture, not one of Werner's more successful items.

I also participated in the Lake Placid Film Forum for a while. They invited me to present their Career Tribute award to a couple of fine filmmakers, Miloš Forman in 2000 and Norman Jewison in 2001, and I moderated panels with the likes of Cliff Robertson, Buck Henry, William Kennedy, and Russell Banks, who was a founder of the event, which had a strong literary slant. And in recent years my son Craig has been a leader of the White River Indie Film Festival, aka WRIF, in White River Junction, the Vermont town where he's lived after relocating from Manhattan and Brooklyn a while back. I'm on the selection committee, and the digital age has made the process mighty different from the screening-room sessions and VHS cassettes of my NYFF days.

I'm sure you've known many people who ran major festivals.

I've had quite a collection of acquaintances in the domain of festival chiefs, so let's stick to the ones I worked with directly. I've mentioned my New York Film Festival friends Richard Peña, Joanne Koch, and Wendy Keys, and we've talked about the Montreal festival, where the head was Serge Losique, one of the least popular of the bunch. I always got along fine with Serge, but he was widely considered to be pushy and manipulative. The directors of the Toronto festival during my years of going there were first Helga Stephenson and then Piers Handling, both terrific people, wonderful companions, and first-rate festival organizers. I was equally fond of Alan Franey at Vancouver, the third major Canadian festival.

I first met Hans Hurch from Vienna when we served together on an American festival jury, and he then invited me to the Viennale in Austria, where I had a fine time; it's very sad that he died of heart failure at the young age of 64. I was equally fond of Mark Fishkin at the Mill Valley festival near San Francisco. Nat Chediak ran the Miami Film Festival for quite a while, and I should certainly mention three Telluride heads: Tom Luddy, who was also very active in movie production until he died in 2023; Bill Everson, a major film collector who was my prof for a while at NYU; and Bill Pence, who was a Dartmouth prof. Good guys all. My longtime New York colleague Kathleen Carroll was a founder of the Lake Placid Film Forum, along with Russell Banks, the gifted writer whom I got to know while participating in that event. There's also Jed Dietz, the very convivial gent who ran the Maryland Film Festival in Baltimore until his retirement in 2018, whereupon the festival collapsed for a while, although it's up and running again now. I'll also mention Sundance Film Festival head Geoff Gilmore, another chief who wasn't very popular with some critics, and I'm pretty sure he steered me to some films not because they were the best on display but because he wanted another body in the audience for a second-rate item. I'm sure I'm forgetting some of the others I've known over the years, but those I've mentioned should suffice.

Have you done any film programming outside festivals?

I'm doing that every time I choose films for one of my classes. But more to the point, I have fond memories of my time with the Makor/Steinhardt Center of the 92nd Street Y in New York, where Ali Siegler invited me to work on a new Major Speakers Series supported by special funding they'd received. Ali and I would discuss possibilities for guests and films, and I'd coordinate many of the logistics. We had evenings with Steve Buscemi, Richard Linklater, Wim Wenders, Mary Harron, and Terry Zwigoff and Daniel Clowes, always with a screening of the filmmaker's latest picture. As we were approaching the end of the series, I got an unexpected offer to have Robert Altman, one of the great American filmmakers, and Garrison Keillor, then a major cultural celebrity, speak at a screening of *A Prairie Home Companion*, based on Garrison's hugely popular NPR show. It was one the last hurrahs for Bob, who died later that year.

   I also did presentations at Makor not connected with that series. The most memorable was when I hosted an evening devoted to *Capturing the Friedmans*, Andrew Jarecki's first-rate documentary about the family of a convicted pedophile. The pedophile dad had died before the film was made, but his son Jesse Friedman, who was also charged with pedophilia, is an important figure in it. This event was supposed to be moderated at Makor by my friend Harvey Roy Greenberg, who's both a psychiatrist and a film scholar, but Harvey decided that appearing in public displays was part of the Friedman family's pathology, and declined to participate. I had no professional scruples along that line and readily stepped in. I had first met Andrew at Cannes, so we knew each other a bit; he joined me and Jesse on the stage, and I also met Jesse's brother David, who was in the audience. It was an altogether fascinating event.

Another activity I should mention is the cinema-club scene, an under-recognized part of film culture. I've already mentioned Talk Cinema, founded by Harlan Jacobson after he left the editor's chair at *Film Comment*. Like similar clubs, it sells season subscriptions, and members see new movies that haven't yet opened in theaters, at least not locally. There's also a host and frequently a guest to give background on the film and answer questions from the audience. I was host, guest, or both at Talk Cinema venues in Manhattan, Philadelphia, and various other places, and for a while I had my own chapter at the BAM Rose Cinema in Brooklyn. Along the way I've been a guest at quite a few other clubs, and for many years I was the regular host of the Cinema Club at the historic Avalon Theater in Washington, DC, owned and operated by Andrew Mencher. When the Covid-19 pandemic hit, Andy had to close the club, and I miss it. I think the pandemic largely decimated the cinema-club world.

TEACHING, EDITING, BOOKS

Along with being a film critic, you've been a professor for many years. How did that come about? Was it always part of your plan?

Long-term plans aren't my strong point, so no, this wasn't some sort of long-term goal. When I was in high school and college I thought I might end up a high-school teacher, although that wasn't a career I particularly aspired to, and I was rescued from it by getting into journalism. I did think I'd be suited to teaching, since I was reasonably smart and liked to talk, but I hadn't been to graduate school, so getting a university job was an unlikely prospect.

But a friend of mine was Renée Shafransky, a writer and sometime filmmaker I first met through my friendship with Spalding Gray, her boyfriend and briefly her husband. Renée was an adjunct professor at the C.W. Post Campus of Long Island University, and when she decided to move on—she left the job to produce the movie *Variety*, directed by Bette Gordon, also a friend of mine—she asked me if I'd like to give it a shot. She recommended me to the department chair, who interviewed me and gave me the position. From the get-go I was teaching three courses per semester, which is a full load at most colleges, but my *Monitor* job gave me enough time flexibility to handle it. Another friend was Annette Insdorf, a film professor at Columbia University, and when I'd been at LIU for a year or so I asked her if Columbia might have something for me. She said there was little available in film studies if you didn't have a PhD, and I didn't at that time, but then a vacancy arose and she said I could fill it by co-teaching a course—Introduction to the Study and Theory of Film—with Richard Peña, who was already an adjunct there. Richard only had a master's degree, but he was running the New York Film Festival, which was obviously a fine credential, so he taught two thirds of the course and I taught one third. Very soon after that I was invited to teach on my own, starting with the Silent Screen course, dealing with early cinema.

I liked teaching, and I liked the income it provided. Then too, curiosity had led me to do a lot of reading in the realms of film theory and history, so I was fairly well versed in the academic material. On the downside, I was less than enchanted with my LIU students, who tended to be nice young people without much intellectual sophistication. Looking at my first batch of term papers, I was appalled at the bad grammar, awful spelling, and all-around inarticulacy on page after page. Was this the state of "higher education" in the modern age? Evidently it was, at least outside the elite universities, so I set about improving my status by embarking on long-de-layed graduate study. Columbia had recently shuttered its doctoral program in film, and I had to stay in New York for my *Monitor* work, so the Cinema Studies department at New York University was my grad school of choice. I started on my MA at the beginning of 1990, when I was in my middle forties, and I finished my PhD at the end of 1993. During those years I paused my LIU teaching, but I worked for the *Monitor* as always, and taught many Columbia courses too. It was a very busy time!

I should add that I greatly enjoyed NYU while I was there; going to grad school meant reading the same sorts of heavy tomes I'd been reading anyway, but having people right there to answer questions and talk about things. That said, however, there were plenty of disappointing aspects. One of my profs was the notorious Annette Michelson, a brilliant scholar whose reputation for being a prickly, crotchety curmudgeon was amply justified. She never gave me any trouble, and it was fun attending seminar sessions in her apartment not too far from the campus, but she could unload in mighty aggressive ways on someone who showed up insufficiently prepared or otherwise rubbed her the wrong way. I mention her because once when we were chatting she said how unhappy she was that cinema studies had been devoured by cultural studies—that the aesthetics of cinema were now taken far less seriously than the socio-political implications of cinema. She was absolutely right, and I shared her misgivings. Like her I was deeply interested in politics, but I wanted to explore cinema as an art first, a sociocultural phenomenon second.

Yet many of the classes and seminars were so fixated on the racism, classism, sexism, and heteronormativity of mainstream films that I sometimes felt I was in a commu-nity of cinemaphobes whose main response to movies was suspicion and hostility. I also disagreed with the prevailing methodology in the advanced seminars, which often allowed semi-informed grad students to drone away while the professor, who really knew this stuff, tolerantly listened instead of cutting to the chase with comments rooted in years of experience.

Individual professors could also be a bit dodgy in their attitudes and practices. The illustrious film historian Robert Sklar became a friend, but when I suggested Bergman's highly experimental *Persona* as the topic for a presentation in one of his seminars, he didn't like the idea, saying people didn't talk much about Bergman in the Cinema Studies Department anymore—as if the academic fashion of the moment should be a deciding factor in choosing subjects to research. I also asked Bob to be on my dissertation committee, and in the year I spent writing it I succeeded in getting a grand total of one meeting with him, during which he had virtually no suggestions to offer. Another odd character was Bill Simon, who was then chair of the department. He was also on my committee, and I didn't manage to get even one meeting with him; then when it was time for me to defend the dissertation, I couldn't get him to confirm that he'd show up at the appointed time. He did show up in the end, but he put me through some real suspense, and another prof on my committee said this sort of thing had happened before. At the other end of the spectrum was Bob Stam, my dissertation advisor. He was prompt, efficient, and helpful from first to last.

The bottom line about my NYU experience is that I met, interacted with, and befriended some very fine folks there, but on the intellectual level I now think a lot of that time didn't pay particularly high dividends. I did emerge with the academic credentials I was after, and since one of my goals in going to grad school was to surround myself with more sophisticated students than the LIU crowd, it's more than a little ironic that I was soon more entrenched at LIU than ever. My friend Lucille Rhodes was a longtime film professor there, and she launched a campaign to get me a full-time position, starting at the associate-professor level. It worked, and after the usual try-out period I became a tenured full professor.

Some of the students were woefully underprepared for college: one asked me what the word "images" meant—and yes, English was his first language—and another had no idea how to use the index of a book. But the film majors at least liked movies, and it was fun exposing them to films they wouldn't have looked at on their own. I once introduced a screening of Warhol's eight-hour *Empire* at the American Museum of the Moving Image, and one of my students was among the few people in the audience! She wasn't there when the film ended, but neither were any of the others who'd been there at the beginning—maybe the seats just weren't comfortable enough?

Along the way I joined a faculty group at Columbia called the University Seminar on Cinema and Interdisciplinary Interpretation, an incredibly ponderous name; when I told Stan Brakhage about it, he said it sounded like a lung disease. This is one of many faculty seminars administered by a central Columbia office, and I've been invited to speak at some of the others—the Seminar on Death, the Seminar on Religion, the Seminar on Moral Education, the Seminar on Love Studies—as well. Our film group met once a month in Faculty House at Columbia, and I served as co-chair with William Luhr, a fine scholar of film noir and Blake Edwards, among other topics, from 1999 to 2005 and again from 2010 to 2015. I owe my friendships with Bill, Gilberto Perez, Harvey Greenberg, Krin Gabbard, and many other kindred spirits to my years with the Seminar, to which I still belong.

So things stayed very busy, since I was still the *Monitor* film critic and still teaching numerous courses as a Columbia adjunct. But by this time my life was changing in other ways, and I decided it was time to slow down and take more control of my own schedule. I took early retirement from both the *Monitor* and LIU in 2005 and moved to Baltimore, where my then girlfriend and later wife was on the full-time faculty of the Maryland Institute College of Art, teaching courses in literature, psychology, and related areas. I joined MICA's adjunct faculty and have been happily ensconced there ever since.

Books

When did you write your first book?

In the early 1990s I wrote a negative review in the *Monitor* of Ray Carney's book *American Dreaming: The Films of John Cassavetes and the American Experience*. Ray got in touch about it, thanking me for reviewing the book and for speaking in such positive terms about John's films, which we both greatly admired. Some time later, Ray told me he was starting a new series called the Cambridge Film Classics at Cambridge University Press, a series of "skinny volumes" that would analyze key films of important directors. He asked my advice about filmmakers to include and possible writers of the books, and I sent him a pretty long and detailed list of suggestions. He was extremely grateful, and invited me to write on a filmmaker of my choice. I first thought of Jacques Rivette, whose work had been written about less than the other New Wave directors, but then I looked at Ray's own list of filmmakers to include and saw that Alfred Hitchcock wasn't there. This seemed to be a glaring omission, but Ray wasn't fond of most Hollywood directors, since he found their work too polished and calculated—he favored roughhewn, intuitive directors like Cassavetes, Mike Leigh, Barbara Loden, and their ilk. I loved Hitchcock, and when I suggested writing about him, Ray said yes.

The series format called for close readings of five or six films, so I selected *Blackmail, Shadow of a Doubt, The*

Wrong Man, *Vertigo*, *Psycho*, and *The Birds*, followed by an epilogue dealing mainly with *Marnie*. The writing went smoothly, and when Ray sent me the edited copy of my first draft, I was delighted with how few changes or emendations he asked for. Then it went to the publisher, and Ray called to say that the editor there, Beatrice Rehl, loved it. A long delay followed, since Cambridge wanted to release the first five books in the series simultaneously, and the others weren't ready yet. When they did appear, *The Films of Alfred Hitchcock* quickly became the bestseller of the bunch and soon went into a second printing. Beatrice then asked me if I'd expand it for a new edition, saying they'd launch with considerable ballyhoo, but I was way too busy, so I declined, a decision I still regret. Not long afterward Cambridge cut way back on film books, so if I do prepare a revised and expanded edition I'll have to peddle it somewhere else.

That's the story of my first book, and since my experience with Ray and Cambridge had been pleasant, I proposed another volume for the series. They had just rejected someone's manuscript on Jean-Luc Godard, so I jumped on the opportunity. Books in the series were getting longer, so the Godard project could be more expansive. Once again I chose six films, from *Breathless* in 1960 to *Nouvelle Vague* in 1990, plus a chapter on JLG's video and television works. As research for the project I dug up a lot of interviews with Godard, including one of my own, and I published a number of them in an edited volume for the Conversations with Filmmakers series that my friend Peter Brunette was editing for the University Press of Mississippi; later I did a similar Mississippi volume on Robert Altman, and then Lucille Rhodes and I edited a collection on Terry Gilliam, a recent friend of mine and a good friend of Lucille, who'd been close him for decades.

In the early 2000s my editor at UP of Mississippi, the wonderful Seetha Srinivasan, invited me to assemble a collection of my critical writing, which became *Guiltless Pleasures: A David Sterritt Film Reader*. My other books came about in different ways. Two of them, *Mad to Be Saved: The Beats, the '50s, and Film* and *Screening the Beats: Media Culture and the Beat Sensibility*, published by Southern Illinois University Press in 1998 and 2004, were drawn from my doctoral dissertation, and years later I wrote *The Beats: A Very Short Introduction* for Oxford University Press. I wrote *Spike Lee's America* when Polity Press asked me for a contribution to its America Through the Lens series, and although a colleague told me that a White critic writing about a Black filmmaker was asking for trouble, I never heard a murmur of objection when the book came out. My book on *The Honeymooners* was written for the TV Milestones series at Wayne State University Press. *Rock'n'Roll Movies* was for the Quick Takes series at Rutgers University Press. *The Cinema of Clint Eastwood* was for the Directors' Cuts series at Wallflower Books, which was folded into Columbia University Press while I was writing it. That covers most of my books, and there may be more to come.

The Beats

Do you still keep up with criticism and scholarship on the Beat Generation, after writing three books and numerous essays and articles about them?

That's an area I think I've done enough on, but I still have some interest in the subject, and I'm on the editorial board of *The Journal of Beat Studies*, although it's a while since I've written much on the Beat crew. It all started when I was looking for a topic for my PhD dissertation in the early '90s. Checking through NYU's index of scholarly writing on film, I was surprised to see almost nothing about the Beats, who had always intrigued me for their experimental spirit and for their subversive attitude to postwar American culture, which wasn't as monolithically conservative as people often believe. Think of the wilder forms of rock'n'roll and the profane comedy of Lenny Bruce as well as the writing of the Beats, especially Allen Ginsberg's supercharged poetry, Jack Kerouac's spontaneous outpourings, and William S. Burroughs's fragmented prose and freewheeling obscenities.

Since my field was cinema studies my dissertation needed a cinematic focus, and that included both mainstream movies and avant-garde films. I turned the bulk of my dissertation into my book *Mad to Be Saved: The Beats, the '50s, and Film*, and used some of the other material for *Screening the Beats: Media Culture and the Beat Sensibility*. They came out in 1998 and 2004, respectively, and since then I've written on the Beats for *The New York Times*, *The Journal of American History*, and various other venues. I've also done a bit of Beat-film programming at Lincoln Center.

Who are the best Beat writers, in your opinion?

For me the best is Ginsberg, whose poetry often has a vigor and propulsion and verbal pungency that are truly electric, especially when you hear him read it aloud. I met him during my Boston University days, when I was film critic of the BU newspaper. He asked me if I'd seen Warhol's *Chelsea Girls*, which was just coming out, and when I said I hadn't caught it yet he assured me it was "funny," which is one of many adjectives you can apply to it. I also remember a joint reading he gave at BU with his father, Louis Ginsberg, also a poet but a far more traditional one who believed strongly in rhyme and other time-tested qualities. Someone asked the elder Ginsberg what he thought about Allen's fascination with psychedelics, and he said something to the effect of "he tells me that when he takes these drugs his mind flies free of its shackles and roams with ecstasy through the vast spiritual reaches of the infinite cosmos. And I say, "Allan, take it easy!'" That got a great laugh from the audience.

Kerouac's best writing is marvelously poetic, and he can come up with words that seem exactly right even though they aren't really words. At other times his prose can be sort of clumsy, although he certainly has a gift for terrific titles — *On the Road*, *The Subterraneans*, *The Dharma Bums*, *Tristessa*, *Desolation Angels*, *Doctor Sax: Faust Part Three*, et cetera. Even his first novel, *The Town and the City*, is pretty good in a very conventional way. He might have been one of the great American novelists if his whole adult life hadn't been sunk in alcoholism.

Burroughs was brilliant in bits and pieces, but the brilliance is very real. I don't relate much to the sexual fantasies and over-the-top exoticism of his more linear novels, but the grimly luminous images of *Naked Lunch* and the other cut-up novels are remarkably powerful, and I'm fascinated by the gnostic mythos that underlies his most interesting work. He had unique gifts. In contrast with Ginsberg, though, I can take just so much of his spoken voice in movies and documentaries where he talks. Such a monotonously droning tone!

What films do you examine in the books?

Commercial films touching on the Beats include *The Subterraneans*, based on Kerouac's novel of that title, and *A Bucket of Blood*, a Roger Corman quickie about a Beatnik coffee house and its resident psychotic. And there are less directly Beat pictures like *Young Man with a Horn*, with Kirk Douglas as a trumpeter based on the pre-Beat but legendary Bix Beiderbecke, and *Paris Blues*, with Paul Newman and Sidney Poitier as American jazz musicians abroad. More recently there's been Walter Salles's *On the Road*, which is okay but doesn't amount to a whole lot, and Michael Polish's excellent *Big Sur*, also based on Kerouac's experiences. Also a good documentary-fiction hybrid, *Howl*, made by the team of Rob Epstein and Jeffrey Friedman and focusing on the obscenity trial of Ginsberg's superb poem.

John Cassavetes's *Shadows* is a pioneering independent picture that falls between the commercial and avant-garde categories. It had an ironic early history with Mekas and company. Jonas loved it, and *Film Culture*, which he had founded with his brother Adolphus Mekas, gave it the magazine's first Independent Film Award. But Cassavetes, a maverick even by maverick standards, decided it needed much more work, so he reshot and reedited it, changing it so drastically that Mekas reversed his high opinion, now calling *Shadows* an ordinary Hollywood-type movie. The revised version still ended with a text describing it as "an improvisation," but that version was far more scripted and rehearsed than the first one had been. Cassavetes despised labels and would never have called himself a Beat, but *Shadows* embodies the Beat spirit—in its loosely plotted narrative and its roughhewn performances and the jazz by Charles Mingus on the soundtrack.

The quintessential avant-garde Beat movie is *Pull My Daisy*, by the photographer Robert Frank and the painter Alfred Leslie, and Ron Rice made some films full of the Beat spirit, notably *Chumlum* and *The Flower Thief*. Antony Balch's *The Cut Ups* and *Towers Open Fire* are both inspired by Burroughs, who also did the narration for Balch's rejiggered version of the Swedish film *Häxan* from 1922. More broadly, the whole New American Cinema group, spearheaded by Jonas Mekas and promoted by New York City institutions like the Film-Maker's Cooperative, the Filmmakers' Cinematheque, Anthology Film Archives, and *Film Culture* magazine, all of which Mekas helped found, shared the Beat ideal of changing human consciousness by way of challenging and undermining received forms of wisdom and behavior. Key filmmakers there included Stan Brakhage, Maya Deren, Kenneth Anger, Barbara Rubin, Jack Smith, Gregory J. Markopoulos, Lionel Rogosin, Andy Warhol, Frank and Leslie, and Mekas himself. In all, the Beats are best served in the avant-garde films that share their anarchic, experimental spirit. Back in the '70s Ginsberg showed up so ubiquitously in underground movies that I used to say there must be a statute requiring every avant-garde filmmaker to include him in a least one shot! Commercial movies rarely capture them very effectively, though. Cronenberg's *Naked Lunch* is a bold try that fizzles out, and John Byrum's

Heart Beat, a biopic about Kerouac and Neal and Carolyn Cassady, is flat-out boring. One amusing detail I've noted is that while Ginsberg wasn't what most people would call a handsome man, he was played by the movie-star likes of James Franco and Daniel Radcliffe on the screen.

Editing

Tell me about your experiences as a magazine and journal editor.

First let's talk about some of the significant film magazines. During my early years as a critic, there were a few periodicals aimed at moviegoers looking for thoughtful and literate commentary. *Film Culture,* edited by Jonas Mekas and devoted largely to avant-garde cinema, influenced me by covering films that were difficult to see but worthwhile to know about, and when I was able to watch many of those films—by Kenneth Anger, Jack Smith, Andy Warhol, etc.—I had a head start in understanding them.

Three other magazines were more widely available and had a more lasting presence for me in later years. I've already mentioned *Film Comment,* where I eventually wrote numerous film reviews and did an interview with the great Iranian auteur Abbas Kiarostami that was a highlight of that period for me. Unfortunately, the magazine ceased publication in the post-Covid era. *Film Quarterly,* published by the University of California Press, recruited me for occasional book reviews, and then editor Rob White and book editor Matthew Bernstein invited me to be the chief book critic, a job I kept for quite a few years. Things changed when Rob abruptly vanished from the scene—just up and abandoned the editorship without a word of warning. The press called me and asked if I'd take over, which was a nice vote of confidence in me. I had just taken early retirement from my full-time jobs and was reluctant to take another permanent post, but I agreed to serve as guest editor while they looked for a new permanent editor. That lasted a couple of years, and eventually they settled on B. Ruby Rich for the job. I'd known Ruby for years, and after being guest editor I co-edited a couple of issues with her before stepping down and leaving things in her hands. After doing all I could to keep the publication on its feet and to ease her into the editor's chair, I was quite surprised when she promptly replaced me as chief book critic and didn't even keep me on the magazine's editorial board. Shabby behavior, in my opinion. Very, very shabby. In any case, I've lost interest in the publication since that time.

Cineaste is the third and best of these magazines. It was founded by Gary Crowdus, who runs the show to this day, and I started contributing to it in the '90s, doing DVD and Blu-ray reviews, book reviews, and long-form articles as well. This became a regular setup and I was invited to become an official contributing writer. I admire *Cineaste* for its stable of gifted contributors, its emphasis on both the aesthetics and politics of film, and its impeccable editorial standards. I write a DVD or Blu-ray review for every issue and often a second one for the magazine's website, and also I do a fair number of book reviews and feature articles—examples of the latter include surveys of Fritz Lang's silent films, Jerzy Skolimowski's early work, John Farrow's under-recognized career, and Louis Feuillade's elegant crime serials.

You've been a journalist, an author, a professor, a speaker, a chair of critics groups, and a TV and radio commentator. Have these activities been interconnected for you?

As touched on earlier, none of this was part of some planned-out strategy. These are things that many critics do, although not many go the professor route, which requires academic credentials. I think of this in a sort of Ptolemaic way. At the center of the system are the people who make films, and the others—movie reviewers, film-studies teachers, media commentators, et cetera—spin around them in their own little orbits. I've been one of the orbiters.

Styles

How would you describe your writing style? Do you write differently in regular reviews and in academic essays? Do you adapt your style to the medium?

I've been both a journalist and an academic for decades, and these days I most enjoy writing for *Cineaste*, which is positioned comfortably between the two—thoughtful enough for deeply engaged cinephiles, readable enough for people who just find movies interesting and fun to think about. At their best, a magazine like this brings reviewing and criticism into smooth alignment. The key thing for writing in any venue is to keep the prose as clear and readable as possible. Few things irritate me more than writing on *any* subject that shows more interest in display and showing off than in conveying ideas in a lucid, communicative manner. Of course the vocabulary I use in a scholarly essay, and to some extent the syntax and overall structure, are different in some ways from what I'd be likely to use in a magazine article or newspaper review, but clarity and communicativeness are still crucial goals.

When doing interviews, do you adjust your approach according to the reputation and/or temperament of the subject—for instance, someone said to be bad tempered or hostile, or someone who doesn't like journalists?

I suppose I tread more carefully if someone has a reputation for being unpleasant to interviewers. I once had a session set up with the towering filmmaker Luis Buñuel when he was visiting New York, but someone else interviewed him a day or two earlier, and word came down that he'd gotten so angry with something that journalist said that he stalked out of the room. It was doubtful that he'd continue with the rest of his scheduled interviews, but the publicist said I could try to talk with him at a party being given in his honor by John and Faith Hubley, the great animators. It was worth a shot, so I showed up at the Hubleys' apartment, and there was Buñuel, and I had a sudden vision of saying or asking the wrong thing, whereupon he would again stalk out and ruin the event for everyone, so I decided not to chance it. My trepidations won the day.

On the flip side, I've had some terrific interviews and found out later that the person was known for being prickly or difficult with interviewers. A couple of choreographers were in that category: Twyla Tharp, who was very forthcoming while wolfing down a meal after a performance, and Lucinda Childs, who was a breeze to converse with.

Back to the subject of reviewing, have you ever written a sentence or a phrase with the aim of being quoted in movie ads?

I certainly hope not! Doing that is infra dig in the reviewing trade—writers who aim at the ads are derided as "quote whores," an impolite term but sometimes an accurate one. More broadly, I'm more and more unhappy about film criticism serving as an advertising and public-relations tool. Reviews have been quoted in ads since the dawn of time, and some people may decide to see a picture because they like the critic or they like a word or phrase in the quote, but that's clearly not a reliable way of selecting one's viewing pleasure. And nowadays the internet is crammed with puff pieces, celebrity stories, burblings about cult favorites, gushing by unsophisticated enthusiasts, and the like, ad infinitum, ad nauseam.

All this stuff appeared in fan magazines of old, much of it fabricated by the studios to promote their products and stars, but you could escape it by simply not picking up the magazines. Now it's pretty much unavoidable online, at least for people like me whose line of work becomes a magnet for those particular algorithms. And it isn't only films that suffer these indignities—my feeds are full of clickbait about orchestra conductors, opera stars, theater productions, and so on. One good thing about academic criticism is that it's not conducive to quoting in mass-market ads!

And since I just used it, let me add that the term "cult movie" really turns me off. When it means anything at all, it's usually an excuse for bad filmmaking. Some people love bad films—maybe they enjoy feeling superior—but not me, and I have zero tolerance for bad movies as a source of derisive laughter. Of course some films are risibly awful, but seeking them out in order to deride them is a foolish waste of time. You and I once gave papers at a conference on "Trash Cinema" at UC Berkeley, and the conference screened a couple of allegedly trashy films—*The Tingler*, which isn't bad at all, and *Dr. Goldfoot and the Bikini Machine*, if memory serves—equipped with noisemakers for the audience to hoot and squawk with. Not enlightened practice, in my view. Nor do I have much patience with camp or campy movies, which are also a case of turning poorly made culture into material for a dubious form of connoisseurship.

CRITICAL COLLEAGUES

Which critics have been most important for you? Which do you respect most?

I've already mentioned Arthur Knight's book *The Liveliest Art*, which bored me as a teenager. Back then I looked at newspaper and magazine reviews in a casual way, but when I started getting more serious, one of the critics who interested me was Dwight Macdonald, who wrote for *Esquire* and disliked almost everything he saw, or so it seemed to me. I was amused when the magazine published a letter from a reader saying they should stop making poor Macdonald go to the movies—nobody should suffer so much! But his no-nonsense opinions made an impression on me.

I first noticed Pauline Kael when her essay "Zeitgeist and Poltergeist; Or, Are Movies Going to Pieces?" came out in *The Atlantic* in 1964. I was still in college, but her reverse snobbism has bothered me ever since, and she sometimes confuses critiquing a movie with critiquing the audience or critiquing another critic. I found her personally very pleasant, and she was always a lively and readable writer. But her habit of rounding up troops of writers to echo her own views is not my idea of sound critical practice, and her opinions aren't necessarily as well grounded as her aggressive prose makes them appear. I've always thought her constant use of the second-person *you*—the movie makes *you* think, the story makes *you* wonder, the actor makes *you* feel—has a touch of bullying about it. On the upside, though, she can be very funny.

As for other critics, my opinions vary. I have never agreed with the common view that James Agee is some sort of critical titan, since his reviews tend to be fairly terse, which is fine, but also telegraphic and sketchy, geared more to consumer-guide brevity than to thoughtful analysis. And there are times when he expresses different opinions about the same topic in articles for different publications—divergent reviews of Laurence Olivier's *Henry V*, for instance, and unsteady opinions about the merits and demerits of color cinematography. Defenders of Agee say that contradictions like these show how challenging it is to write for different publications with different readerships, but I think that's a manageable task if you handle it with care. On the other hand, longer pieces, such as his famous essay on silent-film comedy, can be quite illuminating. He was a very fine screenwriter, too, and like Pauline, he could be funny. In his defense, it's worth recalling that he deemed himself a "would-be critic" and an amateur, taking "amateur" in its original sense of "lover" of an art, and as such he's a commendable figure.

Some of the books I found interesting in my early years include *Films and Feelings* by the Canadian critic Raymond Durgnat, and W. R. Robinson's edited collection *Man and the Movies*, which has an essay by R. H. W. Dillard about horror movies that I thought was quite nice, although I'm not sure how it would strike me today. In the '70s I was impressed by James Monaco's books on *The New Wave* and *American Film Now*, and by *Hollywood Films of the Seventies* by Philip Dray and my friend Seth Cagin. I also liked the first edition of *Transcendental Style in Film: Ozu, Bresson, Dreyer* by Paul Schrader, whom I got to know pretty well later on. The revised edition is also good, with interesting reflections on slow cinema and other timely subjects. Those are the books I chiefly remember now from that period, although there were surely others that intrigued me.

I've learned a lot from Sarris, as I've said, although he was much better as an auteur theorist than as a week-to-week reviewer. I've also learned a good deal from his wife, Molly Haskell, the most essential pioneer of feminist film criticism. Sarris was terminated from the *Village Voice* in 1989 by Howard Feinstein, who had recently become film editor there. Howard was a close personal friend of mine, but I think cutting Sarris loose was a foolish mistake, bad for the *Voice* and bad for cinema, even though Andy found another berth at the *New York Observer*, a minor paper where he shared the movie beat with Rex Reed, a lovely guy but an unrepentantly nonintellectual critic. Howard also published a very long and very negative article about the New York Film Festival during my time on the selection committee there, and it could be a tad tricky navigating my friendships with both Howard and Joanne Koch, the NYFF executive director and a chief target of the article, which was motivated largely by Howard's rage at her for ousting Richard Roud from his leadership of the festival. Personal politics can play a regrettable part in film culture, sad to say.

And so can personality quirks. As much as I respect Andrew Sarris's contributions to American film criticism, he occasionally rubbed me the wrong way. There was a major revival of the first *Star Wars* movie in the '90s, for instance, and rather than dust off my opinions and rehash that familiar territory, I got the idea of asking a few other critics for brief takes on the film, about 75 words each, which I'd compile into an article, thereby saving myself from a boring bit of writing. I was at a film festival with Andy and

Molly—I think it was the Sarasota festival of French film, where both of them were on a panel I chaired—and they both readily agreed to my *Star Wars* proposal when I asked them. But when I followed up back in New York, the first thing Andy asked was whether he'd be paid, and when I said no, he refused, and he refused on Molly's part as well. For a measly 75 words! Seems kind of chintzy to me.

Sarris was replaced at the *Voice* by Jim Hoberman, his longtime second-stringer and a truly top-flight critic. His byline is J. Hoberman, and when I asked him why he chose that, he said nobody ever called him "James," and "Jim" sounded too informal. Very reasonable! He's one of the perilously few mainstream critics to have a firm and deep understanding of avant-garde cinema, and he's equally eloquent as a reviewer of art pictures and commercial movies. His commitment to independent cinema is so strong that he wrote a very interesting book on Yiddish film, *Bridge of Light*, in the early '90s, and Yiddish cinema is as independent as they come. Jim also pays close attention to the politics of movies, writing from a strongly left-wing perspective without getting preachy or doctrinaire.

Roger Ebert became far and away the most famous American critic thanks to the TV show—itself a game changer for movie reviewing—that he and Gene Siskel did for many years. Gene knew what he was doing, of course, but Roger was truly born to be a movie critic. I realized this when I first knew him and we walked out of a screening room together. The film had ended about a minute earlier, and I asked him what he thought of it, and he gave a completely formed answer in perfectly formed sentences, talking about a movie that was scarcely over! If ever a critic had a calling for the trade, Roger was that critic.

I often saw him and his genial wife, Chaz, on the festival circuit, and he was always a pleasure to trade opinions with. Not that I always agreed with him, of course. I remember having lunch with him and a few others at Cannes after the screening of Roberto Benigni's *Life Is Beautiful*, about a man who uses humor and clowning to protect his little boy's innocence when they're both incarcerated in a Nazi concentration camp. Humor can have a place even in a Holocaust film, as Lina Wertmüller showed in *Seven Beauties*, probably her best picture. But for me *Life Is Beautiful* is appalling, utterly false as psychology and sadly demeaning as history. I brought it up at the lunch table and was surprised to hear Roger jump to its defense. And so did my longtime friend Annette Insdorf, who had written *Indelible Shadows*, one of the definitive books on Holocaust cinema—she found the movie a celebration of improvisation and quick thinking. I'm all for improvisation and quick thinking, but I part company with the defenders of Benigni's scurrilous film. That aside, Roger was a truly gifted critic, and he managed his horrible, ultimately fatal cancer with a courage and goodwill that I fear I could never equal. He allowed awful parts of his daily maintenance to be filmed for Steve James's documentary about him, *Life Itself*, sharing his private ordeal with the world at large, and when he was no longer able to eat, he wrote a cookbook! What a guy.

I've already mentioned the admirable Stuart Klawans, who reviewed movies in *The Nation* for years and served with me on the NYFF selection committee. He's a superb writer, one of the best in the business, and his opinions almost always ring true even when I don't wholly agree. I'll also mention three film critics for the *New York Press*, a small weekly that eventually bit the dust. I saw them regularly during my New York years, and I took a deeper dive into their work when I reviewed *The Press Gang: Writings on Cinema from the New York Press, 1991-2011*, a thick volume of their articles, for *Cineaste*. Matt Zoller Seitz has a special gift for pithy formulations, writing that Spielberg's *The Terminal* is "like Capra doing Kafka" and that Quentin Tarantino's *Kill Bill: Vol. 1* makes him wonder if "archivist directors [are] the cinematic equivalent of singer-songwriters with a sense of history, or has the unsuspecting viewer wandered into karaoke night?"

Armond White is one of the scandalously few African-American critics to achieve a major mainstream reputation, and although I've liked him enormously for years, and I certainly value his perspective as a gay Black critic, I've had many hesitations about his writing—he's an incorrigible contrarian who loves to raise a ruckus and doesn't hesitate to insult his readers, other critics, and even whole countries, as when he denounces Australia and New Zealand as "third-rate cultures." But the *Press* collection immersed me in his writing for many hours, showing me that he's a much more complex and thought-provoking writer than I'd realized.

The third of the *Press* critics is Godfrey Cheshire, a good friend who balances solid reviews of art films and commercial releases with carefully cultivated expertise on Abbas Kiarostami and Iranian cinema in general. He doesn't always suffer bad movies gladly, and I vividly remember when he scrambled out of our row midway through a press screening of the appalling *Patch Adams*, muttering "Life is too short!" I stayed put, but I totally sympathized with him. As for his views, he can be brave in going against the grain of current fashion. Writing about the 1996 Sundance festival, for instance, he writes that straining for diversity in the program "meant several really terrible films about this year's favored subgroups, lesbians and Native Americans. It did not mean... any films boosting the identity politics of Southern Baptists, polar explorers, insurance salespersons, Michigan militia men, *Playboy* centerfolds, Republican presidential candidates, Hare Krishnas or Richard Petty fans. Diversity being best, presumably, when it's not too diverse." I stand with Godfrey on that.

When you were writing for the Monitor, *did you have a competitive relationship with other critics at other outlets, or was it usually friendly?*

Pretty much all of us got along well, and I wouldn't describe any of our relationships—my relationships, at least—as competitive. There may have been rivalries or animosities that escaped my notice, but if so, they were buried pretty well. That said, there were one or two critics who could be belligerent in print, going beyond the usual differences of opinion that are part of the profession.

I've already mentioned Armond White, who took pleasure in being a contrarian and is easily the feistiest critic I've known, apart from John Simon, and John's most aggressive words were directed at people he was reviewing, not other members of his profession. A good example of Armond's ornery side is on display in a *New York Press* article from 2011, when he chaired the New York Film Critics Circle and presided over the banquet where our awards were presented. Certain colleagues of ours found remarks he made from the podium to be antagonistic or downright rude, and Jim Hoberman of the *Village Voice* and Lisa Schwarzbaum of *Entertainment Weekly* went public with their dissatisfaction over this. Armond struck back, writing that Jim and Lisa were "class oppressors" and "shills" motivated by "racism." Lisa was "shameless" and "indecent," with a "pathetic, vindictive need to manipulate film culture," whereas Jim was a "real despot" acting on "sinister whims." Et cetera. Yikes! Reviewing the collection of *New York Press* reviews that concluded with this article, I opined that this was pretty rich coming from a critic who had written a few months earlier that "when film discourse becomes discourteous, mindlessness takes its revenge on reason." An interesting point. Armond should have applied it to himself.

Did you have any hesitations about criticizing Armond for the attacks he made in his article?

Nope. After quoting his article in my review of the book for *Cineaste*, I wrote that I didn't mean to diss Armond the way he dissed those colleagues, but hey, he really brought it on himself. I added that he may have regretted those words when he had cooled down, but I think every critic—every journalist, for that matter—would probably like to retract some words written in the past. I know I have some poorly considered prose lurking in whatever archives there may be, and I hope it's allowed to stay in the obscurity where it belongs.

Armond liked raising ruckuses, and I can't think of anyone else who shared that predilection, at least to that extent. Most of the New York critics—and most American critics and critics from other parts of the world, judging from the many I've known—have been judicious in their relationships with colleagues. I think this is a good thing, and it's also good that critics don't tend to gang up, either to support particular movies or directors they like or to put down ones they don't like. Once again there are exceptions—the most notable was the network of Paulettes, the reviewers Pauline Kael would cajole in phone calls, doing her best to line them up in whatever direction she wanted the discourse on a movie to take. I remember a meeting of the NYFCC when Morgan Freeman won as best supporting actor for *Street Smart*, and the vote was so quick and smooth that it seemed prearranged. Which it undoubtedly was, by Pauline and her telephone. But by and large, we're a pretty independent-minded bunch.

Are there any critics whose opinions baffle you, or seem inexplicable?

I'm not sure about bafflement or inexplicability, but the *New Yorker* critic Richard Brody has almost become a reverse barometer for me—our bottom-line opinions about films are diametrically different surprisingly often. He seems to like film after film after film, or rather he seems to *adore* film after film after film, including those that deserve far more restrained and far more nuanced opinions. I got to know Richard personally when he joined the National Society of Film Critics during my time as chair, and I've sometimes run into him in Baltimore, since he was an enormous fan of the Maryland Film Festival, which was indeed a nice festival in its heyday, although not remotely as spectacular as his writing made it sound. I've found his opinions to be savvy and sophisticated on some occasions, weirdly off base on many others. In all, he's a peculiar case.

Has another critic ever influenced your opinion of a particular film, or even turned you around on a movie?

Yes, it's happened, but more often it's been a question of a colleague broadening my view or just helping me learn more about a picture. Years ago my friend John Anderson and I co-edited *The B List*, a collection of essays on B movies, and around the same time I wrote a *Huffington Post* article responding to the question of "who needs critics?" I'll quote the end of my article, where I said that editing the essays on B movies "brought one revelation after another. A piece about *The Rage: Carrie 2* made me realize it's not only spookier than *Carrie*, it's also 20 times more intelligent. It hadn't occurred to me that the right-wing space opera *Red Planet Mars* can be read as an allegory of the Rosenberg spy case, and I'd forgotten that Nicolas Cage actually *eats that cockroach* in *Vampire's Kiss*! In print or online, it takes a natural-born critic to dig out the overlooked facts and ingenious interpretations that my *B List* colleagues have surprised me with time and again. So who needs critics? I do. And so does everyone who cares about movies."

Once in a while I've been challenged about an opinion in a way that was memorable even if it didn't change my bottom-line evaluation of the movie in question. Years ago on a *Monitor* television show I debated David Brudnoy, a conservative pundit very well known in the Boston media world, about Oliver Stone's terrific film *JFK*. I regard that movie as an extended thought experiment, geared to stimulating thought rather than establishing well-grounded facts, and I repeated Oliver's statement that it presents a "counter-myth," laying out a set of alternative ideas about a subject already encased in mythologies. David jumped on me, implying that I was making excuses for the film's own ideology, and he asked whether I'd accept a counter-myth about Martin Luther King that similarly went against the grain, skewing its narrative in ways that contradicted my preexisting view of the great African-American activist. That took me by surprise, and I must admit that David had a valid point—not about the movie, which I still rate highly on both political and cinematic grounds, but about my not-very-sophisticated defense of its basic ideas. That was certainly a learning experience for me.

Did you critics hang out together or socialize personally, or was that mainly at film festivals and on committees? Are you personally close to any fellow critics?

I was something of a workaholic in my New York years, and I used to say that in the regular course of things my most frequent socializing was talking with colleagues before and after screenings. At festivals, though, there would be a good deal of eating and drinking at lunch and dinner, with the drinking mainly after the day's last film or interview. The festival with the most regularized social life was the World Film Festival in Montreal, where the festival housed us at the Hotel Meridien, a large hotel with a spacious lobby. Pretty much every evening we critics would start to gather, pulling up a few chairs around a table, and as the evening progressed the chairs would get more numerous and the circumference of the circle would grow. That was unusual, since at most festivals the critical corps would stay in multiple hotels or apartments. The Montreal festival was far from the best in terms of programming, but those evenings were marvelous.

This is a good a place for a word about Pierre Rissient, who didn't run a festival but was a ubiquitous presence on the festival scene. We first met at Cannes, when he came up and addressed me by name and started chatting. I had no idea who he was, although I had seen him around and noticed that he never wore formal dress even at formal Cannes events. Soon after that I asked some friends about him, and they described him as a *éminence grise*, which is exactly right. I got to know him very well, and he had connections with every festival and personality you could think of—he'd even been Godard's assistant back in the *Breathless* days. His obituary in *Variety* said Clint Eastwood's nickname for him was "Mr. Everywhere," and that's just the moniker I would have given him.

As for critics who have been particularly close personal friends, I'll start with Peter Brunette, who was also a long-time cinema scholar; he and another friend, David Wills, did a lot of work on Jacques Derrida and film philosophy. Peter died at only 66 years old, and he made a dramatic departure from life, succumbing to a heart attack while having breakfast at an Italian film festival—according to the person at the table with him, his head sank onto his chest and it took a moment for the other person to realize he hadn't simply fallen asleep. With his mordant sense of humor, Peter would have appreciated the joke that went around after his death. It seemed a good way to die, passing peacefully away at a film festival, so how could it have been even better? If it were twenty years later, and *after* breakfast.

Other good friends have included Stuart Klawans of *The Nation*, John Anderson of *Newsday* and elsewhere, and David Ansen of *Newsweek* and now the Palm Springs film festival. I also have warm feelings about the late *Time* critic Richard Schickel, and about Molly Haskell and Andrew Sarris, tremendously important contributors to the field. In an adjacent area, my closest museum friends have included several Museum of Modern Art savants—Mary Lea Bandy, Larry Kardish, and Jytta Jensen, as well as Mary Lea's husband Gary, a painter, and Larry's partner Jillian Slonim, another fine cinema person.

Among academics, Tom Doherty is a terrific historian and a terrific guy to talk and hang around with. Ditto for Stephen Prince, but in the past tense, since he died at 65, far too young. And I have great affection and respect for Wheeler Winston Dixon and Gwendolyn Audrey Foster, two erudite and prolific film scholars. Gwendolyn has written extensively on cinema and race, class, sexuality, and other socio-cultural areas, and is a filmmaker as well. Wheeler has written and edited a remarkable number of books and is also a filmmaker with a wide-ranging body of movies to his credit. And among other activities, Wheeler and Gwendolyn were co-editors of *Quarterly Review of Film and Video* for many years before I took on the job. They are exceptionally versatile and productive talents.

ACTORS, GENRES, MOVIE MUSIC, RUNNING TIMES

Let's talk about actors. I know you have favorites and bêtes noires.

And a lot of people in between. Acting has always been one of the most undertheorized areas in film studies, although I wrote an article on screen performance in postwar Hollywood for a collection edited by Claudia Springer and Julie Levinson, and James Naremore wrote a very solid book on the subject. It's different in journalistic reviewing, where critics have few inhibitions about tossing out opinions, and a reviewer like John Simon will freely insult an actress' face or figure as if they were mistakes of craft or misuses of talent rather than natural attributes over which one has little control. I'll mention here that I knew John for many years, and I also knew Sylvia Miles, and one of her finest hours came in the early '70s, when John dissed her appearance in a play. Shortly afterward she ran into him at a restaurant and proceeded to dump a plate of food on his head! The incident sums up both personalities nicely.

One of the most common clichés about acting is that it's nearly impossible to explain why one actor makes a strong impact or demonstrates star power while another, no less physically attractive or skilled in technique, doesn't make the grade. And the cliché is pretty much true. This is why Hollywood has almost invariably demanded a screen test—putting the actor in front of a camera and checking out the footage—before offering a role or finalizing a contract, even if the actor seems to have all the necessary goods offscreen. There are indeed mysterious factors at play, giving some actors speedy, lasting success while relegating others to quick decline at best, instant oblivion at worst.

So it's not surprising that quirks of personal taste loom particularly large when critics opine on screen performances, and that goes for me as well as my colleagues, although I try to balance my gut responses with attention to the craft and expertise on display, however much or little of those there may be. Some top Hollywood stars rope me in as much as they magnetize the general public; my favorites from the studio era include James Stewart, Spencer Tracy, Cary Grant, and James Mason among the men, and Greta Garbo, Barbara Stanwyck, Ingrid Bergman, and Katharine Hepburn among the women.

If I had to single out the greatest of all, I'd go for Stanwyck and Jimmy Stewart, two terrific actors with enormous amounts of sheer star power. Stewart was a brilliant romantic lead in his early years, but after serving as a bomber pilot in World War II, he felt a need to go beyond the largely frivolous roles that had propelled his career in the '30s, deepening his persona in pictures like Hitchcock's *Vertigo* and Anthony Mann's *The Naked Spur*, powerful and intelligent films with powerful and intelligent star performances. My politics are pretty much the opposite of Stewart's right-wing ideology, which was so strong that when I interviewed him in the '70s, he wanted to know if I had American-made batteries in my cassette recorder! But his screen persona was irresistible. Stanwyck was also amazingly versatile, taking in the darkness of Wilder's *Double Indemnity*, the effervescence of Sturges's *The Lady Eve*, and the pathos of Vidor's *Stella Dallas* without missing a beat. She wasn't the most gorgeous of female stars, but she seemed to put her whole self into everything she did, even when the vehicle was second-rate or below. She even did her own stunts on occasion.

I could mention many other stars who were also gifted and versatile actors. Think of James Cagney, who ran the gamut from the singing and dancing of *Yankee Doodle Dandy*, not a very good movie, to the psychopathic gangsterism of *White Heat*, a very great movie. The same goes for Alec Guinness, who was terrific in numerous Ealing comedies, ditto in many David Lean dramas, and iconic in the *Star Wars* series. I have equal respect for Marcello Mastroianni, who could do the comedy of *Big Deal on Madonna Street* and *Divorce Italian Style* as well as the drama of *La dolce vita* and *La notte* and the shifting moods of *8½*. Other obvious choices include Marlene Dietrich, Burt Lancaster, Elizabeth Taylor, Tony Curtis, Shelley Winters, et cetera. Special mention goes to Sidney Poitier, a groundbreaking Black actor with tremendous range and unstoppable charm, which I experienced first-hand when I interviewed him. And no one shines more brightly than Denzel Washington, a towering actor and, from my own brief encounters with him, a very nice guy.

To shift the focus a bit, there are also stars I admire for their skill and energy but find less personally appealing than my favorites. Sylvia Sidney and Ida Lupino don't turn me on, although Lupino was a tremendous creative force in American movies. Bette Davis always has a slightly grotesque vibe—as does Joan Crawford, although a little less so—but this didn't stop them from having stellar careers, and eventually *What Ever Happened to Baby Jane?* arrived to make grotesquerie a major asset. On the male side of the equation, Clark Gable and Victor Mature sometimes seem like caricatures of themselves, to me at least.

Shifting the focus yet again, there are actors I adore for reasons I can't really explain. I first noticed Edward G.

Robinson in *Hell on Frisco Bay* when I was about eleven, and I thought he was kind of ugly but really fun to look at. I still hold the latter opinion. Charles Coburn is like an ideal grandpa. Joseph Cotten is smooth and likable. Natalie Wood is gorgeous. Ann Sothern captivated me in her '50s sitcom *Private Secretary*. Ray Milland has the looks of a classically handsome man… and the list goes on.

Beyond the big stars there are character players who appear and reappear in role after role after role. Agnes Moorehead never disappoints, and in *The Magnificent Ambersons* she gives one of the screen's truly indelible performances. Thelma Ritter and Eve Arden are inimitable, as is Ruth Gordon, who has her greatest field day in *Rosemary's Baby*. Dean Jagger made a lasting impression on me decades ago in movies like the sci-fi quickie *X the Unknown* and the Elvis Presley vehicle *King Creole*, and I've had a soft spot for the minor-league Whit Bissell ever since *I Was a Teenage Frankenstein* in 1957; he was also in *I Was a Teenage Werewolf* that year, but I didn't catch up with that one until later. Judith Anderson, William Demarest, George Sanders, and Peter Lorre are all high on my list, and in today's movies there's Tilda Swinton, an actor of astounding versatility, and Lili Taylor, so versatile that she could play Marilyn Monroe and Abraham Lincoln and be equally convincing in both roles.

Whoopi Goldberg, John C. Reilly, Joan Cusack, Kathy Bates, Benicio Del Toro, Dianne Wiest, William H. Macy, Christopher Walken, Brian Cox, Steve Buscemi, and Raul Julia are also among the finest talents of recent years, equal to any of the topline stars who get their names above the title. I also have to send a mash note to the so-called sissies and milquetoasts of the studio era. Eric Blore is a nonstop delight—his work in *The Lady Eve* is one of the all-time-great comic performances—and Franklin Pangborn, Grady Sutton, and Edward Everett Horton are just as marvelous, as are Victor Buono and the underrated Laird Cregar in more serious roles. Secondary actors like these often acquire cult status nowadays, but their contributions to Hollywood deserve a full measure of mainstream celebration.

Back to the subject of acting in general, I had an illuminating interview with Lee Strasberg, co-founder of the Group Theatre in the 1930s and head of the Actors Studio for three decades starting in the early '50s. He said his goal was to solve "the acting problem," which is basically a question of consistency—one night the actor gives a great performance, the next night it's not so good. Hence the need for a Method to keep the good work flowing. Strasberg turned to the Russian theorist Konstantin Stanislavski for answers to the puzzle, modified by his own ideas and the thoughts of other smart observers. His own approach stressed the internal dynamics of Stanislavski's technique, calling for actors to access their emotional depths by summoning up "sense memories" from their personal histories; he de-emphasized Stanislavski's call for detailed observation of the exterior world, although some Method actors do prepare for their portrayals by spending extensive time with real-life counterparts of the character types and social milieus of the roles they've taken on. Strasberg insisted that the proof of the Method's wisdom was in the success of many of its adherents—it was the public, not the Actors Studio, that made people like Paul Newman, Ellen Burstyn, Julie Harris, and Al Pacino into long-lasting stars. Not to mention Marilyn Monroe, a Strasberg protégée whose acting became increasingly mature as her storied career and ill-destined life moved from modest beginnings to explosive fame and terminal unhappiness.

Strasberg told me that skillful Method actors don't seem to be acting, or parroting lines, or "speaking well," but rather to be talking and behaving in ways so authentic and spontaneous that spectators often confuse the actors with the characters they're playing. Seeking psychological realism on stage and screen became a powerful trend in the years after World War II, when the idiosyncrasies and eccentricities of a Marlon Brando or a James Dean partly supplanted the traditional charisma of a Grace Kelly or a Cary Grant. When I teach on this topic, I say that the old idea was for actors to move gracefully and speak smoothly, no matter how scruffy or downbeat the character may be, because the polished traits of the skilled performer are what audiences want to see; the newer idea is for the actor to disappear into the character as much as possible. Speaking personally, I take great pleasure in the old-style charisma of Cary Grant and William Powell and Laurence Olivier and John Wayne, as different as their individual styles are, and I take equal pleasure in seeing Robert De Niro disappear into Travis Bickle in *Taxi Driver* or Paul Newman disappear into the title character of *Hud*. The actor's persona never goes away, of course, but the character takes over the foreground, and the effect is terrific when it's done well. When it's done badly, on the other hand, overacting, inauthenticity, and showing off can be just as off-putting as in more traditional performances. And some actors want nothing to do with Method techniques. No less a star than George C. Scott heaped scorn on actors who "smear their own hangups over a role," as he derisively described the process, and one great director—it might have been Jean Cocteau, but I'm not sure of that—said that if the actor's left profile is being filmed, it's fine for the actor to ignore inner emotions and sense memories and cry from the left eye alone. Still and all, an impressive list of actors, from Jack Nicholson and James Earl Jones to Dustin Hoffman and Meryl Streep, have put the Method to productive use. What counts is how the actor's choices work for me as a spectator.

I talked about this with Shelley Winters in the early '80s, and she was very articulate about her respect for the Method as an intellectually and artistically serious approach. After reaching a high level of celebrity—thanks largely to *Oklahoma!* on Broadway and *A Place in the Sun* onscreen—she set about studying the Method and teaching at the Actors Studio and elsewhere, motivated by her concern that fame and fortune can be fleeting if you don't have a firm grasp on the inner workings of stage and film performance. That strikes me as a practical and admirable attitude. (But the remark I enjoyed most was her capsule summary of how her screen image had shifted with age—she started out as a sexpot, she said, and now she was a sex oven! Nicely put.)

Genres

Do you have favorite film genres, or is it always a matter of the individual film, the director, and so on?

There's no genre that guarantees good movies or bad movies, but there are some I gravitate toward more than others.

Let's go through some of them.

Horror and science fiction

I've liked horror films since my early teenage years, and I have enormous respect for the classics—the great Universal films of the '30s, the Val Lewton cycle of the '40s, and the Hammer pictures of the '50s, to name a few. Italian *giallo* often gets lumped in with horror but is really a thing apart, and I've never worked up much enthusiasm for it, although Mario Bava's color cinematography can be amazing and some individual productions, such as Dario Argento's *Suspiria*, are impressive. So is Luca Guadagnino's remake of *Suspiria*, by the way. Nowadays the field is overstuffed, and even the most glowingly reviewed horror items are often disappointing or worse, but I retain my respect for superbly crafted and genuinely haunting pictures like *Rosemary's Baby* and *The Shining*.

On a related note, whether or not they fit neatly into the horror genre, certain films sort of horrify me, and I make no apology for despising them. Ruggero Deodato's *Cannibal Holocaust* is Exhibit A in this department; years ago you wrote very well on its complexities, but for me nothing outweighs its unconscionable treatment of animals. Lucio Fulci has done some interesting work, but *The New York Ripper* is way too nasty for comfort, as is Wes Craven's first feature, *The Last House on the Left*, which shows no hint of the inventiveness he shows in some of his later films. As you know, it's not a question of violence per se that turns me off in pictures like these—the mayhem in Michael Haneke's *Funny Games* is highly effective, morally and cinematically, and Gaspar Noé's *Irreversible* is both insanely violent and philosophically rich. Like humor, acceptance of screen violence is a very personal thing. I think I have good reasons for drawing lines where I do, but others may easily disagree.

Science fiction is a near neighbor of the horror genre, and a classic like *Frankenstein* fits neatly into both categories, with a horror-movie monster created by a science-fictional obsessive scientist. Some popular science-fiction novels are among my all-time-favorite reading experiences—the first two novels by Alfred Bester, *The Demolished Man* and *The Stars My Destination*, are masterpieces—and a few science-fiction films are every bit as brilliant and innovative as the best SF literature. To begin at the beginning, Georges Méliès's pioneering silent movies are amazing to this day— the most famous is *A Trip to the Moon*, but there are plenty of others—and no less a modernist than Terry Gilliam has acknowledged their influence on him. Fritz Lang's sprawling *Metropolis* also has enduring value, and his slightly later *Woman in the Moon* has what's probably the first rocket-launch countdown in cinema history. Moving on, I first saw *Forbidden Planet* at age twelve, and its terrifically intelligent concept—monsters from the id, unknown to the very mind from which they spring—made an instant and lasting impression on me even before I realized that the picture is a witty variation on Shakespeare's *The Tempest*. Wise's *The Day the Earth Stood Still* is notable for its humane antiwar message. *2001: A Space Odyssey* stunned me when I saw it in 1968, although I've never much liked *A Clockwork Orange*, one of Kubrick's lesser works. Andrew Niccol's *Gattaca*, Alex Garland's *Ex Machina*, and Spielberg's *A.I. Artificial Intelligence* are also unusually smart genre pictures, and I admire some movies made with little more than mass entertainment in mind—*Close Encounters of the Third Kind*, the extremely witty *Star Trek IV: The Voyage Home*, and *Star Wars Episode IV: A New Hope*, which had the short and snappy title *Star Wars* when it first arrived.

Comedy

I have great affection for comedy, an enormous genre. To start with the silent era, the greatest silent-film comedians do extraordinarily inventive things with their physical actions, which can be positively acrobatic, and with facial expressions and body language, and with the props they handle and the environments they inhabit. I agree with the conventional wisdom holding that Buster Keaton was the most ingenious filmmaker among them, and also the most acrobatic of the bunch—he actually broke his neck doing a stunt for *Sherlock Jr.*, and lucky him, the damage was so limited that it wasn't discovered until years afterward. *Sherlock Jr.* is one of his best films, although my favorite is *Seven Chances*, where he outruns huge boulders cascading down a hill.

Many critics consider Chaplin a lesser filmmaker, concerned less with the possibilities of the medium than with capturing his virtuoso performances, but his directing went far beyond that, albeit in subtle ways—in *Modern Times*, for instance, the image of factory-worker Chaplin rolling through the gears of a large machine is echoed in the overhead view of nightclub-waiter Chaplin churning through a crowd of dancers with a circular tray in his hands. Good stuff!

Harold Lloyd deserves all possible acclaim for his hair-raising acrobatics in *Safety Last!* but he also developed a warm and amiable screen persona—very different from Keaton's marvelous stone face—and he worked well in sound cinema, as his fine acting in Preston Sturges's *The Sin of Harold Diddlebock* amply demonstrates. Harry Langdon is the weirdest of the bunch, a bumbling child-man long before Pee-wee Herman hit the scene. And my favorites definitely include Laurel and Hardy, who started in the silent era and then created splendid comedy in sound pictures, where their vocal tones and acting were as funny as their physical actions. Their movies aren't always great, but the two of them invariably are.

As for comedy after the silent era, I've always found the label "screwball comedy" uncomfortably vague, but the best of those pictures are delightful. Hawks's *His Girl Friday* and *Bringing Up Baby*, Sturges's *The Lady Eve* and *Sullivan's Travels*, and Lubitsch's *Design for Living* and

The Shop Around the Corner are among the greatest, and performers like Cary Grant, Barbara Stanwyck, Henry Fonda, Ginger Rogers, William Powell, and Katharine Hepburn did some of their most memorable work in this genre. The post-screwball era produced the prolific careers of Mel Brooks, whose films are generally too noisy, vulgar, and overbearing for my taste—everyone shouts and hollers all the time!—and Woody Allen, who has created many smart and funny comedies as well as some that are pretty awful. The good ones include *Take the Money and Run*, *Annie Hall*, *Zelig*, *The Purple Rose of Cairo*, *Radio Days*, *Vicky Cristina Barcelona*, and *You Will Meet a Tall Dark Stranger*. The bad ones include *Celebrity*, *The Curse of the Jade Scorpion*, *Whatever Works*, and *Rifkin's Festival*, mostly but not entirely from the later stages of his career. I also like the bittersweet pairing of comedy and tragedy in *Crimes and Misdemeanors*, and it's fascinating that Woody has returned to the theme of unpunished transgression in *Match Point*, *Cassandra's Dream*, and *Coup de chance*.

I've interviewed Woody—even made him laugh a little—and he's very articulate about his work. As an actor, he grants that he has a very narrow range, but feels he can do as well as anyone within that range, which I think is accurate. And when I asked him why a movie like *Annie Hall* incorporates such a hefty number of cinematic devices— voiceover, animation, jump cuts, and so on—he said the world that produced the old silent-film comedians was a highly physical world that called for highly physical humor, whereas the workings of today's electronic and digital world are virtually invisible, calling for different kinds of comic expression. I think that's an interesting argument. Making a movie every year for decades has understandably resulted in misfires and mistakes, but Woody's overall record of achievement is high, especially when you figure in the personal travails he's had to deal with in the '90s and after. In many ways he's a unique screen artist.

Melodrama

Critics and scholars have devoted countless words to melodrama, which is a tricky category because it encompasses everything from tearjerkers, soap operas, and so-called women's pictures to hugely intelligent works by auteurs who use the genre instead of letting it use them. The great Mexican director Arturo Ripstein told me he makes melodramas because it's the basic pop-cultural language of his country. For melodrama at the highest level, a good case in point is the body of work directed by Douglas Sirk at Universal-International in the 1950s. The first time I saw *Imitation of Life* it struck me as pure soap opera, superficial and sentimental all the way, and it can easily seem that way if you judge by the screenplay alone. But the more I studied it, and the more helpful guidance I got from my friend Fred Camper and the other smart thinkers who introduced me to Sirk's films, the more subtlety, intricacy, and expressive power I was able to see in what I increasingly regarded as a true aesthetic masterpiece. I don't place every Sirk film of the '50s on the same lofty plane, but the best of them— *Imitation of Life*, *All That Heaven Allows*, even the comic *Has Anybody Seen My Gal*—have my very highest regard.

And the virtues of these films are rooted in Sirk's own creative personality as well as the genius of the production system. They are both mass-audience weepies and sharp-eyed dissections of contemporary social issues, and Sirk had the intellectual depth and cultural savvy to pull off this difficult balancing act. So did Rainer Werner Fassbinder in his best work, such as *Ali: Fear Eats the Soul*, which is a remake of *All That Heaven Allows* with higher stakes, bringing racism and ageism into the picture. And so does Todd Haynes from time to time—his *Far from Heaven* is another remake of the Sirk movie, now with homophobia added to the list of social ills on display. Melodrama can be weak and weary, but in the right hands it can be thoughtful and trenchant.

Processes

While we're discussing movie genres, I'll add a few words about formats and processes, which I've always enjoyed thinking about. I was a young kid when the original 3D wave came along in the '50s. I was exceedingly impressed with 3D comic books, which gave remarkably vivid in-depth images, but it was 3D movies that really intrigued me. I remember seeing the coming-attractions trailer for the first 3D feature to be released, Arch Oboler's melodrama *Bwana Devil*, which my parents regarded as too grownup for little-boy viewing. Decades passed before I finally caught up with it on a DVD with a flawed but detectable 3D effect, and although it proved to be a mediocre movie at best, it was gratifying to see the thing at last. My uncle took me to another 3D picture in the '50s—it was *Miss Sadie Thompson*, not a likely prospect for me to enjoy at about eleven years old—and the 3D didn't thrill me much, maybe because my myopia was kicking in and I didn't yet have eyeglasses. Years later I watched some of the major 3D pictures in revival theaters—New York's marvelous Film Forum, for instance—so I've seen classics like *Dial M for Murder* and *House of Wax* in their proper form. I also recall *The Stewardesses*, an idiotic 1969 release that wedded 3D with pornography. I used to say in a semi-serious way that porn is the genre most naturally suited to 3D, but Wim Wenders's 2011 *Pina*, a superb documentary about Pina Bausch and her sensational dance company, made me realize in a completely serious way that dance and 3D are the most simpatico cinematic partners. For a while my Oppo Blu-ray player and plasma flatscreen gave excellent results with 3D discs, but the plasma screen eventually broke down, and new ones are hard to find nowadays. I may seek out another one at some point, and I'm glad to see some video companies experimenting with 3D effects on regular screens. I think the most spectacular 3D experience I've had was seeing the 2015 picture *Everest* in IMAX 3D; the story is a fairly routine mountain-climbing adventure, but the cinematic experience was genuinely immersive. I was also greatly taken with another 2015 release, *The Walk*, about a highwire acrobat traversing the space between the towers of the World Trade Center in my old Manhattan neighborhood. Either despite or because of the fact that I'm an acrophobe, movies about danger in high places often thrill me. I even liked the 2022 picture *Fall*, about a couple of young women scaling a defunct broadcasting tower, and *Skywalkers: A Love Story*, a hair-raising documentary about people who photograph themselves striking precarious poses in (for me) unthinkably lofty places. Yow!

Another new 1950s process was Cinerama. In its original form, it used three side-by-side projectors to display a super-wide picture, and there were very visible seams where the three adjacent images came together on the screen. I didn't see the initial release of *This Is Cinerama*, which introduced the format in 1952, but I saw the film when it was revived years later. In 1958 I saw *Windjammer*, made in Cinemiracle, a short-lived Cinerama competitor, and yep, it had a mighty big screen. As did the epic *Around the World In 80 Days*, which I saw in the absurdly named Todd-AO format at New York's Rivoli Theater in 1956. Hollywood was competing fiercely with the inexorable rise of television, which helps explain the proliferation of formats that provided viewing experiences you couldn't get on the small, mostly black-and-white TV screens of that era. CinemaScope was the reigning champion in this sweepstakes. The first 'Scope release was *The Robe*, which I saw it in its initial 1953 release, and numerous other widescreen formats soon followed.

Goofier formats arrived in later years. One was Sensur-round, a '70s process that used huge subwoofers to shiver your nostrils during kinetic moments of *Earthquake* and *Rollercoaster*. And then there was John Waters's witty use of Odorama, where viewers received a scratch-and-sniff card to deploy at key junctures in the story. The smells were about what you'd expect in one of John's strenuously disreputable productions. And of course William Castle gets a special mention here. He was the great guru of silly cine-matic gimmicks, among which was the immortal Percepto, whereby a teensy shock is administered to the viewer's backside during the scene in *The Tingler* when the epony-mous monster is supposedly loose in the very theater where you're sitting. My old friend Bruce Goldstein wired up half the seats of an auditorium in Film Forum, since he regularly included *The Tingler* in the theater's repertory program-ming, and when he proudly showed the setup to Castle's widow, she wondered why he went to so much trouble. Her late husband just wired a handful of seats, knowing that when a couple of people leapt and yelled *everyone* would have a good time!

Are there any genres or types of movies that simply don't interest you?

There's no broad category of films that I write off—liter-ally or figuratively—as being completely worthless. That said, though, I sympathize with Martin Scorsese's contro-versial comment about comic-book superhero movies not being cinema, at least in the humanistic sense that he takes as a measure of worthwhile filmmaking. When he compares such pictures to theme parks, he's exactly right. Of course they're cinema by definition—they consist of moving pictures on a screen—but they're locked into formulas that privilege superficial action over psychological meaning and value mass-market commerciality over everything. And for me they tend to be flat-out boring. So like Marty, whom I've long considered the greatest living American director, I have trouble relating to them as meaningful uses of this amazing medium. Maybe that's a blind spot of mine. Or maybe it's a clear-seeing spot of mine! Either way, I consider myself in excellent company, with the illustrious Scorsese in the same camp.

Soundtracks

Let's talk more about music. Do you enjoy listening to movie soundtrack music? So much of it is released on vinyl, CDs, MP3s, and streaming platforms.

Soundtrack albums have never been a major enthusiasm of mine, but of course I truly love some movie scores, and I've enjoyed talking with composers like Henry Mancini and Michel Legrand. In the '60s I fell in love with the *West Side Story* score, on both the Broadway original-cast album and the soundtrack album of the 1961 film; the astonishing Leonard Bernstein and Stephen Sondheim are in absolutely peak form there. I'm even more hooked on Duke Ellington's score for *Anatomy of a Murder*, a brilliant use of jazz with some elements bordering on avant-garde music. I still listen to it with tremendous pleasure.

There's delicious music in Truffaut's *Shoot the Piano Player* and *Jules and Jim*, and I love a less celebrated French score, Francis Lai's superb music for Claude Lelouch's *A Man and a Woman*. I admire that whole movie more than most critics do; it's hopelessly romantic, but it gets to me despite its excesses, and Lai's music is an unforgettable part of it. A scattershot list of other great movie composers would include Elmer Bernstein, with classics like Preminger's *The Man with the Golden Arm* and the title music of Dmytryk's *Walk on the Wild Side*, and Mancini, with scores for Welles's *Touch of Evil*, Hawks's *Hatari!*, and multiple works by Blake Edwards: *Days of Wine and Roses*, the *Peter Gunn* TV series, *The Pink Panther*, et cetera. And of course there's Ennio Morricone, a hugely prolific composer who broke new ground for instrumentation and was innovative in all sorts of ways in scores for Sergio Leone and a long, long list of other filmmakers. Yet when I was preparing to interview him I listened to some of the classical compositions he wrote, and they left me cold.

A composer who deserves special mention is Bernard Herrmann, who had a truly remarkable career. His first score was for *Citizen Kane*, his second was for *The Devil and Daniel Webster*, which brought him an Academy Award, and his last was for Scorsese's *Taxi Driver*, a defining movie of its epoch. He worked with everyone from François Truffaut and Brian De Palma to Ray Harryhausen and Robert Wise, and episodes of the classic *Twilight Zone* series are among his many TV credits. But his music for Hitchcock is his best and most deservedly famous achievement. His score for *Psycho* is played entirely by strings, going heroically against the grain of traditional scary-film music, and the score for *Vertigo* is utterly transcendent, with its ascending and descending patterns ("I look up, I look down," says the troubled protagonist) and its gorgeously off-kilter tonalities. He also consulted on the electronic music in *The Birds*. It's a silly exercise, but if I had to name the single greatest movie composer, I'd name Herrmann.

Looking beyond particular composers, I also like the jukebox scores of movies like *American Graffiti* and Floyd Mutrux's underrated *American Hot Wax*, partly because of the nostalgia element, but also because the movies benefit enormously from their rhythms and textures. For me the decisive value in a rock'n'roll song—the classic '50s and early-'60s kind—isn't melody or harmony, which are usually rudimentary, or lyrics, which are usually negligible—but *texture*, the overall sound and feel of the recording, in which all of the above come together, successfully or not, depending on the participants, the engineering, and so on. Those textures become integral parts of the movies that incorporate them, at least when the incorporation is done right. That's a basic idea in my book *Rock'n'Roll Movies*.

Another interesting thing is that for some mysterious reason, rock'n'roll biopics are good surprisingly often— *The Buddy Holly Story*, *Great Balls of Fire!*, *La Bamba*, and plenty more. I've never been into Ike and Tina Turner very much, but *What's Love Got to Do with It* is phenomenal. So is *A Hard Day's Night*, although it isn't exactly a biopic, and Clint Eastwood's *Jersey Boys*, about Frankie Valli and the Four Seasons. Some movies set in later periods, like *Control* and *24 Hour Party People*, are terrific as well. And outside the rock-music frame, there are fine pictures like *La Vie en Rose*, with Marion Cotillard's astounding portrayal of Édith Piaf; Eastwood's *Bird*, about the saxophone giant Charlie Parker; the well-acted *Ray* with Jamie Foxx as the versatile Ray Charles; Karel Reisz's *Sweet Dreams*, about the great country singer Patsy Cline; and Steven Soderbergh's *Behind the Candelabra*, about Liberace, of all people. Not every pop-music picture makes the grade, and while I regard Todd Haynes as a very gifted filmmaker, his *Velvet Goldmine* is overstuffed and his Bob Dylan biopic, *I'm Not There*, strikes me as too scattered.

Dylan's own rock extravaganza, *Renaldo and Clara*, is a total mess but not entirely without merit—the live performance of "Isis" might be the most amazing single song ever caught on film. Years ago I wrote an academic article pairing *Renaldo and Clara* with Frank Zappa's *200 Motels*, a similarly discombobulated spectacle. They're prime illustrations of what I call the aesthetics of incompetence, unpredictable results of people with talent in one field barging into another field where instinct and intuition fill the vacuum left by the absence of actual skill. *200 Motels* was co-directed by Tony Palmer, a real professional, but Zappa's anarchic sensibility gives the picture its texture. A nod also goes to *Cocksucker Blues*, the scrupulously unpolished Rolling Stones movie by the trailblazing photographer Robert Frank. (I'll add that for many years *Cocksucker Blues* was supposedly unavailable for copyright reasons, but I found it without difficulty on a shelf in a Manhattan video store. Another allegedly unseeable film was Frederick Wiseman's first documentary, *Titicut Follies*, about an appallingly run Massachusetts mental institution; patient privacy was used as an excuse to keep the film out of circulation. When I moderated a Q&A with Fred at the New York Film Festival in 1989, I mischievously informed him that I'd gotten a 16mm print of *Titicut Follies* from the New York Public Library by simply showing my library card at the check-out desk. Fred then conceded that the film wasn't *completely* out of circulation. Fair enough, but the movie's legend was modified a bit.)

Getting back to jukeboxes, Marin Scorsese's rock-music soundtracks set the standard in that department. The title of his first feature, *Who's That Knocking at My Door*, has a religious meaning, but the words come from a late-'50s hit by the Genies that's pretty much forgotten now (except by me), and his first major film, *Mean Streets*, is crammed with first-rate rock'n'roll, most daringly when Harvey Keitel staggers drunkenly around a nightclub floor to "Rubber Biscuit," recorded by the Chips in 1956, a preposterously silly song that perfectly matches the character's boozy brain fog. *New York, New York* is about a jazz musician, but the main character was originally planned as a clarinet player, and I think Scorsese changed the instrument to saxophone because the sax is far more important than the clarinet in the pop music Scorsese loves best. "I'm a rock fan," he said straightforwardly when I interviewed him about that picture. There's plenty of rock'n'roll in *GoodFellas*; *The Last Waltz* was a groundbreaking rock-concert movie; and his documentaries on Bob Dylan, George Harrison, and the Rolling Stones are solid entries in the rock-doc canon. On the flip side, though, I admit to hesitations about the music of *The Irishman*. The movie itself is a little wan when measured against Marty's very best, and perhaps for that reason, the rock on the soundtrack is distracting, enhancing the atmosphere but also pushing me away from the narrative. In that context, the music is too engaging for its own good—or rather, for the good of the movie.

Long movies

Critics obviously encounter many bad movies in their work. Why don't you ever walk out of films the way Godfrey Cheshire did when Patch Adams *proved too much to bear?*

My superego, aka my inner movie cop, polices me too closely for that. Apart from special circumstances, such as marathon selection-committee screenings, my policy is always to stick it out. As an earlier reviewer once remarked, the definition of a critic is a person who sits through things. And as the video artist Nam June Paik recommended, you should stay with a movie you hate so you can hate it *thoroughly*.

I'm sure that can be challenging when a film is very long.

As you can imagine, long movies can be highly rewarding or highly irritating, and occasionally both. As a teenager I discovered that a long and excellent novel can build a convincing world that gets inside you and stays with you. James Jones's *From Here to Eternity* was a favorite in that department. The same can happen with lengthy films, the big difference being that you can take a novel at your own pace, whereas a movie takes you at *its* pace, at least if you're seeing it in a theater and not on your own video setup.

What are some the most interesting long movies?

Back in the 1960s I went to see Sergei Bondarchuk's epic Soviet production of *War and Peace*, which runs about six-and-a-half hours, and I left the theater after the first portion. I had a couple of reasons for leaving: I had already watched a full-length movie that morning, and a friend was visiting from out of town. But when a movie was gone it was gone, in the pre-video days, and I always regretting not seeing all of that one. Years later it was released on DVD, so I finally caught up with it, and while it's not a masterpiece, it's a perfectly good adaptation that holds its own with other treatments, including King Vidor's well-done Hollywood version. And the length of the Soviet picture is justified by the length of the novel it's based on, which I've read three times, if memory serves.

There are movies much longer than that, though, sometimes meant to be shown as a string of TV episodes but released in theaters as well. Ingmar Bergman's *Scenes from a Marriage* is one such, existing in a shortened theatrical version as well as a full-length original version. One of the most celebrated long pictures is Rainer Werner Fassbinder's *Berlin Alexanderplatz*, which clocks in at about fifteen hours, even though it's based on the superb novel by Alfred Döblin, which isn't unusually long. I first saw Fassbinder's film in two afternoons at the Museum of Modern Art, and later I renewed my acquaintance via the video edition. It's not one of Fassbinder's very best works, partly because Günter Lamprecht's performance puts me off a bit, but it's a considerable achievement.

Jacques Rivette's *Out 1*, also known as *Out 1: Noli Me Tangere*, is a special case. It's about thirteen hours long, divided into episodes that suggest TV as its logical habitat, but Rivette also made a version running about four and a quarter hours, titled *Out 1: Spectre*, which isn't just a shortened edition but a fully reedited work with its own distinctive structure. I saw *Out 1: Spectre* first, and it was one of the most thrilling film experiences I'd ever had, although the thrill has been milder in later viewings. I've also seen the lengthy *Out 1* more than once, on video, and as Rivette has acknowledged, it has its longueurs. Like some of his other films, it deals with a theater company, and the scenes of actors rehearsing run out of steam well before they're over. It's still a unique and remarkable picture, though. Rivette has made quite a number of long movies, from the somewhat long *Paris Belongs to Us* to the very long *L'Amour fou* and *La Belle noiseuse*—which also exists in a shorter version called *La Belle noiseuse: Divertimento*—and the sheer extensiveness of the films is central to Rivette's project of disrupting and renewing cinema conventions. He was at least as radical as Godard, his prodigiously rebellious New Wave colleague, and my hat is permanently off to both of them.

And then there's *Sátántangó*, the 439-minute drama by the Hungarian auteur Béla Tarr, based on a provocative novel by Lásló Krasznahorkai, who collaborated with Tarr on the screenplay of this and four other Tarr films. I've seen *Sátántangó* theatrically and on video, and while it's not Tarr's best picture—that honor goes to *The Turin Horse*, with *Werckmeister Harmonies* a close second—it's as bold and uncompromising as they come. Other worthwhile long movies are Bernardo Bertolucci's five-hour-plus *1900* and Michael Cimino's three-and-a-half-hour *Heaven's Gate*, which is better in its full-length version than most critics, myself included, gave it credit for when it was new.

Some people might name Krzysztof Kieślowski's ten-part *Dekalog*, inspired by the Ten Commandments of the Old Testament, but I regard that as a series, so it doesn't count as a single film any more than the *Star Wars* franchise does. Then again, I think *The Human Condition*, directed by Masaki Kobayashi, can plausibly be called a single long movie even though it's really a trilogy totaling more than nine-and-a-half hours. I don't think of myself as a macho character, but I've always taken a sort of macho pleasure in confronting and conquering long and demanding films. It's part of the endless diversity that movies can offer.

There are also films I find as ordinary as they are lengthy—various Hollywood epics of the '50s, for instance, often in the neighborhood of three hours, although Cecil B. DeMille's *The Ten Commandments* runs for three hours and forty minutes, and is so un-cinematic that it feels twice as long. Some long movies also fall into the "slow cinema" category, which has been very fashionable in recent years. There are indisputably slow movies that I adore—great films by Andrei Tarkovsky, Aleksandr Sokurov, Tsai Ming-liang, and Apichatpong Weerasethakul among them. But being long and/or slow is not a virtue in itself. I've spent many hours watching many-hours-long and doggedly slow films by Lav Diaz, for instance, and his work lost its spell when I realized how arbitrary some of his gradualist devices are—starting a scene with a view of a distant grove, then running the camera on and on while people emerge and plod across the terrain, all to no purpose except to soak up the ambience, which we've already been steeped in for an hour or two or three. Enough is enough.

Titles

Some of the films you've named—Sátántangó, Out 1, Eaux d'artifice, and so on—have unusual titles. Are you picky about getting titles right?

Picky is what I try to be, but these things can be slippery. A friend once chided me when I referred to a 1974 Brakhage film as *The Text of Light*, saying it was actually just *Text of Light*, but authoritative sources go both ways on that one, and Stan is no longer around to ask. I sometimes have to check whether a title starts with "The" or not. *Sweet Smell of Success* does not, and I've taken note of that. The recent movie adaptation of Colson Whitehead's novel *The Nickel Boys* changes the title to *Nickel Boys*. Go figure.

And there are eccentricities of other kinds—for instance, Lindsay Anderson's *If....* has four dots after the single word. And when I discuss Hitchcock's early film *Murder!* in a class, I jokingly tell students to say the title with emphasis—*Murder!*—because that exclamation point can't be overlooked!

For films made outside the English-speaking world, there's also the question of whether to give a film's original title or the title it's known by in Anglophone markets. Here that's usually decided first by distributors and then by common usage, so items like *La dolce vita* and *Amarcord* are always kept in the original while others are given in translation. But this is complicated by the question of upper-case initials—in English most words of titles have capital initials, while in languages like Spanish and Italian that only goes for the first word. And there's considerable disagreement about correct capitalization in French titles—my understanding is that lower-case initials are used except for the first word, plus the second word if the first word is a brief article or preposition like "le" or "la" or "de," but plenty of people use lower-case for everything after the first word.

On a related note, I mostly resist shortening titles when they're mentioned more than once in an article; abbreviating *Sweet Smell of Success* to *Sweet Smell* or *The Court-Martial of Billy Mitchell* to *Court-Martial* seems lazy, although editors sometimes truncate them anyway. But this is getting into the minutiae of my trade. The minor minutiae, even.

FILM AND PHILOSOPHY

Earlier you mentioned film philosophy. Is that a particular interest for you?

I've written quite a bit in that area, partly because of personal interest and partly because it's been a trend in academic film criticism and analysis. I must say this trend has been somewhat amusing to me. As self-aware academics have occasionally recognized, some cinema scholars have an inferiority complex—they're not part of a centuries-old enterprise like literary criticism or music criticism, and they deal with movies, which are notoriously enmeshed in popular culture rather than high culture. Hence the infatuation cinema scholars fell into for a while with semiotics and psychoanalysis, which allow them to conduct abstruse analyses with the aid of specialized vocabularies and recondite conceptual frameworks.

Then philosophy became all the rage. Some film scholars have real credentials in philosophy—for example, Noël Carroll and my old grad-school prof Allen Weiss, both of whom have two PhDs, one in philosophy and one in cinema studies. And of course there's Stanley Cavell, a major philosopher who has cultivated a thorough knowledge of film over the years, and whom I knew through Vlada Petrić, also a Harvard professor and a close friend of mine. But many others who like to combine philosophy with film studies lack such bona fides.

I studied philosophy a bit as an undergraduate and film-philosophy as a grad student, but that's not the same as undergoing rigorous top-level training. So a growing batch of film scholars became pseudophilosophers with varying degrees of expertise. Around the same time, some real philosophers became fascinated with neurology, becoming pseudoneuroscientists. And that led some film scholars to become pseudophilosophers *and* pseudoneuroscientists, even though their actual credentials were in the far more limited domain of film studies. A funny situation!

One result of this has been a proliferation of film periodicals and books with "philosophy" in the title, and when invited I've contributed to a number of them, my skepticism about the trend notwithstanding. For me it's another way of writing about movies, and I don't claim to be a philosopher in the Cavell or Carroll sense of the term. I used a number of Michel Foucault's ideas and many of Mikhail Bakhtin's concepts in my PhD dissertation and in my book *Mad to Be Saved*, because these were big topics when I was in grad school, but I haven't returned to them much since then. More recently I've written for *Film-Philosophy* and

The Journal of French and Francophone Philosophy and I've contributed essays—or "chapters," as they're called nowadays—for numerous books, writing about *Manhunter* for *Michael Mann and Philosophy*, about Peter Whitehead's *Wholly Communion* for *The Beats and Philosophy*, about *The Informant!* for *The Philosophy of Steven Soderbergh*, and so on. If editors think I'm the person to do these things and they like what I hand in, who am I to argue?

Can you tell about the approaches you use in film-philosophy writing?

A recent essay is a useful example. I was invited to give a paper at a conference marking the sixty-fifth anniversary of Hitchcock's masterpiece *Vertigo*, at Trinity College in Dublin, and the paper I wrote is called "Hauntological Perplexities: Spectrality, Theodicy, and Vertigo," a forbidding title, I admit. A few years earlier I'd written an article on religious imagery for *A Companion to Martin Scorsese*, edited by Aaron Baker, and researching that I'd gotten interested in Jacques Derrida's idea of "hauntology," which has to do with overlaps between past and present whereby specters from the past return to haunt the present, creating ambiguities about the nature of time and of reality itself. The term "hauntology" has also been used in psychoanalytic theory, focusing on deceitful psychic phantoms that haunt and repress the egos they infect.

In a thought process I don't fully recall, I connected all this with Søren Kierkegaard's notion of the dizziness of freedom, a metaphor with clear connections to Hitchcock's film, which is about a man who's chronically afflicted with vertigo and obsessed with a spectral woman who is herself haunted by a guilty past. And finally I returned to issues I'd dealt with before: the lingering effects of Hitchcock's religious upbringing, its relevance to his lifelong fascination with malevolence and death, and the questions of redemption and resurrection that are subtexts in *Vertigo* and in *D'Entre les morts*, the Boileau-Narcejac novel that inspired the movie. So the finished essay, which I read at the conference and revised for an edited collection that's in the works, brings together various ideas from philosophy and theology that I've been mulling over for quite a while. I'm no world-class expert on Derrida or Kierkegaard, but I've read their work over the years, and I know a thing or two about Hitchcock's life and films, and the response to the essay has been favorable, so I guess I've gotten away with it.

I was the respondent when you gave your paper on The Informant! *at Columbia's University Seminar on Cinema and Interdisciplinary Interpretation.*

I well remember! I wrote that for the aforementioned book on Steven Soderbergh, and Steven is such a smart person that it's reasonable to connect him with philosophy. He and I first met when I interviewed him about his second feature, *Kafka*, and we've talked a couple of times since then. I think *The Informant!* is one of his best pictures, and for the essay I went to Deleuze and Guattari's idea of schizoanalysis, which seems appropriate for a film about a man whose grasp on truth, sanity, and reality is so slippery it really seems schizoid, at least in the generic, nonclinical sense of the term.

As you know, Deleuze and Guattari argue that psychoanalysis is "arboreal," rooted like a tree in notions of personal history and family romance that are discoverable by digging into the person's memories, dreams, and free-associating thoughts. But mental activity is actually rhizomatic, according to them, spreading like a vine in multiple directions, forever sprouting new offshoots according to the ever-changing topography of the mental and physical environment. So they replace the static image of an analysand lying on a couch with the dynamic image of a schizo taking a stroll. The hyphenated term *becoming-* is everywhere in schizoanalytic theory—things never just *are*, they're always undergoing change, growth, shrinkage, progression, regression, et cetera, et cetera. I find this a screwy but intriguing notion, in a cultural context if not a clinical one.

The Informant! is based on Kurt Eichenwald's very interesting non-fiction book about Mark Whitacre, a biochemist and wheeler-dealer who embezzled an enormous amount of money from Archer Daniels Midland, the multinational food and commodities company where he worked as a scientist and business manager. The movie is clear about what sets Whitacre apart from the ordinary white-collar criminal—he's a prodigious and gifted liar, inflicting deceptions, equivocations, evasions, and concealments on pretty much everyone who comes his way. He accepts psychiatric treatment, for reasons that are partly therapeutic and partly tactical, but he flummoxes the psychiatrists as well.

I use the clinical definition of "antisocial personality disorder" to describe both Whitacre and the company that employs him, and I use the zigzagging patterns of desire sketched by schizoanalysis as a way of understanding

Whitacre, who's always in a state not so much of *being* but of *becoming*, going with his own mercurial flow like the schizophrenic taking a stroll in Deleuze and Guattari's theoretical scenario. I also connect him with Andy Warhol's claim that his art and personality consist entirely of surfaces with no hidden meaning behind them, and I liken Whitacre's interior monologues, heard in voiceover throughout the film, to the mind-filling jingle in Alfred Bester's science-fiction novel *The Demolished Man*, a piece of viral word-play that jams the mental circuits and flattens the flow of thought into a depthless, deracinated veneer. There's more to the essay as well, but those are examples of the diversified notions that can somehow come together—at least I hope they do—in an argument that more or less adds up. I also gave a version of this paper, leaving out most of the schizo-analytic stuff, at an American Studies conference, slotting the fact-based story into the corporate division of the true-crime genre.

Lacanian psychoanalytic theory has a lot of adherents in academic film studies. Do you often find his ideas valuable, or do you just use them when they're particularly relevant to a topic you're exploring?

Let's say I find some of his notions useful on certain occasions. The same goes for Deleuze, another gnarly philosopher but one with a different psychological orientation: Lacan felt he was returning psychology to Sigmund Freud's essential ideas, whereas Deleuze and his coauthor Guattari, a psychoanalyst by trade, wrote their two *Capitalism and Schizophrenia* books, *Anti-Oedipus* and *A Thousand Plateaus*, from a distinctly anti-Freudian standpoint. Deleuze wrote many books on his own, but I prefer what Žižek wittily dissed as the Guattarized ones, especially the portions dealing with schizoanalysis.

HEADING TOWARDS
THE EXIT

Turning back to your Monitor *career, were the editors surprised when you decided to retire?*

I'm sure they were, because I took early retirement when I was a mere sixty years old. As we discussed earlier, I survived any number of staff cutbacks during the paper's periodical economy drives, so they'd been happy to have me on the staff for well over thirty years. On the other hand, although they didn't say it, I was earning a reasonably good salary by that time, and they surely welcomed the chance to hire someone who'd be less expensive. As things turned out, my replacement was my friend Peter Rainer, who'd written for a number of high-order publications and had a first-rate reputation as a journalist and movie critic. Under their deal he continued working from California, where he'd been based for a long time, and they evidently came to an amicable salary arrangement. So everyone was happy.

What induced you to pull the plug?

Part of it was personal. I'd just been through a contentious divorce, and then I was hit with some contentious post-divorce litigation, and there was a chance that my ex-wife would manage to grab a lot of my future income unless I retired, which was one of the terms of the divorce agreement. A few years earlier this wouldn't have caused me to retire, since much of my work was pleasurable. But the *Monitor* itself was changing in ways that turned me off. As mentioned earlier, they felt their image had been too "elite," a word I heard there all too often, and they were pushing more than ever for movie coverage emphasizing personalities and trendiness and "fun." I thought there was plenty of that in all the other publications out there, and that racing in this direction would hurt the paper's distinctive approach, both in general and in its coverage of entertainment and the arts. At one point they suggested I should stand in front of a theater and talk to people as they left after a movie, which has nothing to do with my idea of being a film critic. And there was the usual simmering disagreement about how many column inches should be devoted to "art films" and the like. So both personal and professional factors were in play.

Then too, I'd been working two full-time jobs for a long time—as a newspaper film critic and a university professor—and I'd sometimes wondered which job I'd give up if I ever decided to slow down a bit. The newspaper job had a higher profile and was more stimulating in many ways, but my tenured professor job had excellent security and wasn't too demanding. Somewhat to my own surprise, I decided to quit them both at once. Along with my full-time jobs I'd been doing lots of other things—freelance writing, speaking gigs, writing and editing books—and now I'd let those activities take over. So I moved from Manhattan to Baltimore, where my partner was a prof at the Maryland Institute College of Art, and settled in there as a writer, editor, adjunct professor, et cetera.

How did the Monitor *announce your retirement?*

They asked me to write an article about it, and I'll quote some of it. Near the beginning I mentioned a question I'm frequently asked: how many movies do I see every week? "I can't accurately answer that," I continued, "since I've never dared calculate the number. I've thought of myself as averaging a movie a day, and a little more if you count old pictures I've revisited for background, research, or (yes) pleasure. So naturally I tremble at the notion of adding this up. It probably comes to some preposterously high number that would prompt some questions of my own: Has this been a good life? Has it been a life at all? Have we reviewers pulled the ultimate scam—getting paid for going to the movies—or have we hoodwinked ourselves by turning a pleasurable pastime into a tiring, time-consuming chore?" For me, of course, the answer has to be "some of both."

A little later in the article I wrote that people curious about reviewing "usually focus on the movie-watching angle, overlooking another part of the critic's job: actually writing reviews. That's when our other activities—watching films, talking with filmmakers, networking with colleagues—must jell into articles that convey not only our opinions of a movie but also the competence of its craftsmanship, its relevance to our lives, the soundness of its ethics, and whether it'll appeal to the reader of today's paper." I wouldn't sum things up in exactly the same way now, but I think that basically holds true. On the most rudimentary level, I've always recognized what I call an idiot optimism in myself. Even after the countless hours of junk, garbage, and dreck I've sat through year after year after year, I always hope the next picture will be one of the good ones. So I keep watching and watching and watching, and every now and then the enterprise pays off.

Did you hear from readers or colleagues when you announced that you were leaving the New York film scene?

Quite a few. One goodbye that stands out in my mind for some reason came from Rex Reed, a famous and not-very-intellectual movie reviewer I'd known for years. He wrote to say I'd always been one of the "good guys," and although that's kind of vague, it touched me. I also received some unsolicited job and gig offers. It all made for a nice sendoff.

As we get to the end of these conversations, would you like to make any final points about your life as a critic or about criticism in general?

I'm increasingly bothered by the ever-growing overlap between movie reviewing and movie marketing. Back in the 1960s, the interesting and eccentric critic Parker Tyler raised the question of whether film criticism was just a form of propaganda, and it's as important an issue now as it ever was. To what extent are critics exploring and explicating films with the aim of informing readers, encouraging thought about the artform, and raising the standard by which movies and other cultural works are judged? And to what extent are they just promoting the pictures they happen to like, boosting their egos by roping others into sharing their opinions? Worthwhile critics do the former rather than the latter, of course, and readers are always free to dispute or ignore the opinions they don't like. But a favorable review is an act of advocacy, and that's inevitably a kind of cultural propaganda, and it isn't necessarily harmless.

As always in modern life, capitalism is at the core of the situation. Woody Allen remarked that movies are the only artform where one of the creative tools is big money, and he was right. Feature films are expensive propositions, and people won't finance them unless there's a fair prospect of good financial returns. Hence the ingrained conservatism of the film industry, which pours its resources into audience-pleasing products as a matter of survival; the only exceptions are the makers of personal and avant-garde cinema, who are marginalized almost by definition.

Audience-pleasing culture can still be deep and excellent if it's created by aesthetically inspired and morally responsible artists. But the older I've gotten, the more irritated I've been by the nonstop barrages of marketing bullshit wrapped around even the most artistically ambitious cinema. I'm glad that the Criterion Collection, the Criterion Channel, the Mubi online platform, and video companies like Kino Lorber and Arrow continue to distribute important films to international audiences. But every movie is pitched as a masterpiece and every filmmaker is pitched as a genius. Enough! To paraphrase some bygone sage, most of everything is crap—more charitably, I'd say most of everything is mediocre—and it's wearing to suffer the endless onslaught of hype that accompanies the good, the bad, and the indifferent without distinction and without letup. Call me a curmudgeon, a complainer, or a grumpy old man, but I think this stuff is harmful, making it harder for viewers, especially unsophisticated viewers, to make reasoned decisions about what to see and to form thoughtful, independent opinions once they've seen it. I realize that it was ever thus—today's cascades of promotional buildup and celebrity gossip are just latter-day versions of the fan-magazine silliness of old—but that doesn't make it right or good.

To conclude on a brighter note, I do not agree with the Death of Cinema crowd. Scorsese is incorrect when he says that today's megabudget comic-book fare isn't cinema—it's made of moving images, so of course it's cinema—but such stuff is irrelevant to what I see as the best, most productive, most world-improving purposes that cinema should serve. To expand on what I said earlier, let a zillion flowers bloom, and let them take a zillion exfoliating shapes and forms, all of them exciting, mind-altering, and bold. Excellent cinema continues to be created, distributed, and exhibited everywhere from neighborhood multiplexes to living-room flatscreens. Our job as critics is to encourage the best of it, discourage the worst of it, and keep the ideas flowing. To return to your very first question, that's as close as I come to having a philosophy of my profession.

BIBLIOGRAPHY

Books

The Films of Alfred Hitchcock (Cambridge Film Classics) Cambridge University Press, 1993. Chinese-language edition, Peking University Press, 2007. Greek-language edition, Publishing House Paratiritis, 1998

Jean-Luc Godard: Interviews (editor) (Conversations with Filmmakers) University Press of Mississippi, 1998. Korean-language edition, Emotion Books, 2008.

Mad to Be Saved: The Beats, the '50s, and Film Southern Illinois University Press, 1998.

The Films of Jean-Luc Godard: Seeing the Invisible (Cambridge Film Classics) Cambridge University Press, 1999.

Robert Altman: Interviews (editor) (Conversations with Filmmakers) University Press of Mississippi, 2000.

Terry Gilliam: Interviews (co-edited with Lucille Rhodes) (Conversations with Filmmakers) University Press of Mississippi, 2004.

Screening the Beats: Media Culture and the Beat Sensibility Southern Illinois University Press, 2004.

Guiltless Pleasures: A David Sterritt Film Reader University Press of Mississippi, 2005.

The B List: The National Society of Film Critics on the Low-Budget Beauties, Genre-Bending Mavericks, and Cult Classics We Love (co-edited with John Anderson) Da Capo Press, 2008.

The Honeymooners (Contemporary Approaches to Film and Television: TV Milestones) Wayne State University Press, 2009.

Spike Lee's America (America Through the Lens). Polity, 2013.

The Beats: A Very Short Introduction (Very Short Introductions) Oxford University Press, 2013. Turkish-language Edition, 2015.

The Cinema of Clint Eastwood: Chronicles of America (Directors' Cuts) Wallflower Press/Columbia University Press, 2014.

Simply Hitchcock (Great Lives) Casa Carlini, 2017.

Rock 'n' Roll Movies (Quick Takes) Rutgers University Press, 2017.

Selected book chapters

"Tennessee Williams, *Cat on a Hot Tin Roof*, and the Movies," in *The Literary Cinema of Richard Brooks*, ed. R. Barton Palmer and Homer B. Pettey. Edinburgh University Press, 2025.

"The Beat Minds of Their Generation," in *The Blackwell Companion to American Literature*, ed. Susan Belasco, Theresa Strouth Gaul, Linck Johnson, and Michael Soto. Blackwell Publishing, 2020.

"*Dutchman*," in *Reading with Jean-Luc Godard*, ed. Kevin J. Hayes and Timothy Barnard. Caboose, 2023.

"*White Mane*" and *The Curse of the Cat People*" and "*Poltergeist*" and "*A Soldier's Daughter Never Cries*," in *For Kids of All Ages: The National Society of Film Critics on Children's Movies*, ed. Peter Keough. Rowman & Littlefield, 2019.

"His Father's Eyes: *Rosemary's Baby*," in *Giving the Devil His Due: Satan and Cinema*, ed. Jeffrey Weinstock and Regina Hansen. Fordham University Press, 2021.

"Robert Altman: Documentaries, Dreamscapes, and Dialogic Cinema," in *When Movies Mattered*, ed. Jonathan Kirchner and Jon Lewis. Cornell University Press, 2019.

"Heroes Are Something We Create: Eastwood's Biopics," in *Tough Ain't Enough: New Perspectives on the Films of Clint Eastwood*, ed. Lester D. Friedman and David Desser. Rutgers University Press, 2018.

"The Beats and Visual Culture," in *The Cambridge Companion to the Beats*, ed. Steven Belletto. Cambridge University Press.

"Ralph Bakshi: De-Disneying Movie Animation" and "David Mamet: Profanity, Flimflam, and the Power of What Happens Next," in *Directory of World Cinema: American Independent 3*, ed. John Berra. Intellect, 2016.

"Breaking the Rules: Altman, Innovation, and the Critics," in *A Companion to Robert Altman*, ed. Adrian Danks. Wiley-Blackwell, 2015.

"Postwar Hollywood: 1947–1967," in *Acting*, ed. Claudia Springer and Julie Levinson. Rutgers University Press, 2015.

"In the Movie-Viewing Machine: Essential Cinema and the 1970s," in *Downtown Film and TV Culture*, ed. Joan Hawkins. Intellect, 2015.

"*The Mahabharata*," "*Cotton Mary*," "*The Unvanquished*," "*The World of Apu*," in *Directory of World Cinema: India*, ed, Adam Bingham. Intellect, 2015.

"Edward Yang," in *Directory of World Cinema: China, Volume 2*, ed. Gary Bettinson. Intellect, 2015.

"Imagery of Religion, Ritual, and the Sacred in Martin Scorsese's Cinema," in *A Companion to Martin Scorsese*, ed. Aaron Baker. Wiley-Blackwell, 2014; rev. ed. 2020.

"Schizoanalyzing Souls: Godard, Deleuze, and the Mystical Line of Flight," in *A Companion to Jean-Luc Godard*, ed. Tom Conley and T. Jefferson Kline. Wiley-Blackwell, 2014.

"Mann and Übermensch: Evil and Power in Michael Mann's *Manhunter*," in *Michael Mann and Philosophy*, ed. Steven Sanders, Aeon J. Skoble, and R. Barton Palmer. University Press of Kentucky, 2014.

"Godard, Schizoanalysis, and the Immaculate Conception of the Frame," in *Sonimage: The Legacies of Jean-Luc Godard*, ed. Christina Stajanova and Douglas Morrey. Wilfrid Laurier University Press, 2014.

Essays on Belgian Cinema, in *Directory of World Cinema: Belgium*, ed. Marcelline Block and Jeremi Szaniawski. Intellect, 2013.

"Wrenching Departures: Mortality and Absurdity in Avant-Garde Film," in *The Last Laugh: Strange Humors of Cinema*, ed. Murray Pomerance. Wayne State University Press, 2013.

Essays on Swedish Cinema, in *Directory of World Cinema: Sweden*, ed. Marcelline Block. Bristol, UK: Intellect, 2013.

Essays on French Cinema, in *Directory of World Cinema: France*, ed. Tim Palmer. Intellect, 2013.

Essays on Indian Cinema, in *Directory of World Cinema: India*, ed. Adam Bingham. Intellect, 2013.

"American Film Criticism," in *Blackwell's History of American Film*, ed. Roy Grundmann, Cynthia Lucia, and Art Simon. Blackwell, 2012).

"*Wholly Communion*: Poetry, Philosophy, and Spontaneous Bop Cinema," in *The Beats and Philosophy*, ed. Sharin N. Elkholy. University Press of Kentucky.

"Representing Atrocity: September 11 Through the Holocaust Lens," in *Hollywood's Chosen People: The Jewish Experience in American Cinema*, ed. Daniel Bernardi, Murray Pomerance, and Hava Tirosh-Samuelson. Wayne State University Press, 2012.

Essays on Chinese Cinema, in *Directory of World Cinema: China*, ed. Gary Bettinson. Intellect, 2012.

Essays on Spanish Cinema, in *Directory of World Cinema: Spain*, ed. Lorenzo J. Torres Hortelano. Intellect, 2012.

"*Pecunia Olet*: Affluence, Effluence, and Obscenity," written with Mikita Brottman, in *Obscenity and the Limits of Liberalism*, ed. Loren Glass and Charles Williams. Ohio State University Press, 2011.

"From Transatlantic to Warner Bros," in *A Companion to Alfred Hitchcock*, ed. Thomas Leitch and Leland Poague. Blackwell, 2011.

"Schizoanalyzing the Informant," in *The Philosophy of Steven Soderbergh*, ed. R. Barton Palmer and Steven M. Sanders. University Press of Kentucky, 2010.

"Morbid Psychologies and So Forth: The Fine Art of *Rope*," in *Hitchcock at the Source: The Director as Literary Adaptor*, ed. David Boyd and R. Barton Palmer. State University of New York Press, 2011.

"George Clooney: The Issues Guy," in *Shining in the Shadows: Movie Stars of the 2000s*, ed. Adrienne L. McLean and Murray Pomerance. Rutgers University Press, 2011.

"Las Vegas: City of the Imagination," in *World Film Locations: Las Vegas*, ed. Marcelline Block. Intellect, 2011.

"Alfred Hitchcock," "All Quiet on the Western Front," "The King of Kings," "King Kong," "Men in Black," "Vertigo," in *Directory of World Cinema: American Hollywood* 2, ed. Lincoln Geraghty. Intellect, 2015.

"Steven Spielberg." "Science Fiction." "*The Day the Earth Stood Still.*" "*Poltergeist,*" in *Directory of World Cinema: American Hollywood*, ed. Lincoln Geraghty. Intellect, 2011.

"Murdered Souls, Conspiratorial Cabals: Frankenheimer's Paranoia Films," in *A Little Solitaire: John Frankenheimer and American Film*, ed. Murray Pomerance and R. Barton Palmer. Rutgers University Press, 2011.

"Spellbound in Darkness: Shyamalan's Epistemological Twitch," in *Spoiler Warnings: Critical Approaches to the Films of M. Night Shyamalan*, ed. Jeffrey Andrew Weinstock. Palgrave Macmillan, 2010.

"A Shadow Poet: Michael Haneke," in *Cinema Inferno: Celluloid Explosions from the Cultural Margins*, ed. Robert G. Weiner and John Cline. Scarecrow Press, 2010.

"That Special Okie Southwest Flavor, That Humor," in *Hal Ashby: Interviews*, ed. Nick Dawson. University Press of Mississippi, 2010.

"Steven Spielberg's Flesh Fair: Film, Fantasy, and Death Denied," in *The Many Ways We Talk about Death in Contemporary Society: Interdisciplinary Studies in Portrayal and Classification*, ed. Margaret Souza and Christina Staudt. Edwin Mellen Press, 2009.

"Ken Jacobs," in *Exile Cinema: Filmmakers at Work beyond Hollywood*, ed. Michael Atkinson. State University of New York Press, 2008.

Dozens of Moments, in *Defining Moments in Film/Movies: The Little Black Book*, ed. Chris Fujiwara. Il Castoro, 2009/ Cassell Illustrated, 2007.

"He Cuts Heads: Spike Lee and the New York Experience," in *City That Never Sleeps: New York and the Filmic Imagination*, ed. Murray Pomerance. Rutgers University Press, 2007.

"Low Hopes: Mike Leigh Meets Margaret Thatcher," in *Fires Were Started: British Cinema and Thatcherism* (2nd ed.), ed. Lester D. Friedman. Wallflower, 2006.

"Fuller, Foucault, and Forgetting: The Eye of Power in *Shock Corridor*," in *Cinema and Modernity*, ed. Murray Pomerance. Rutgers University Press, 2006.

"Festivals" and "Robert Redford," in *The Schirmer Encyclopedia of Film*, ed. Barry Keith Grant. Schirmer, 2006.

"Lumet: Endlessly Energetic," in *Sidney Lumet: Interviews*, ed. Joanna E. Rapf. University Press of Mississippi, 2006.

"*Alphaville: Un Étrange Aventure de Lemmy Caution*," in *Understanding Film Genres*, ed. Sara Pendergast, Tom Pendergast, Steven Jay Schneider. McGraw-Hill, 2006.

"Liv Ullmann: Norway's Glittering Gift to World Film," in *Liv Ullmann: Interviews*, ed. Robert Emmet Long. University Press of Mississippi, 2006.

"Jack Kerouac," in *The Greenwood Encyclopedia of American Poets and Poetry*, ed. Jeffrey Gray. Greenwood, 2005.

"*Irréversible*: The Backward Gaze," in *The X List: The National Society of Film Critics' Guide to the Movies That Turn Us On*, ed. Jami Bernard. Da Capo, 2005.

"The Prisoner of Splendor: An Interview with Harvey Pekar," written with Mikita Brottman, in *Creeping Flesh: The Horror Fantasy Film Book*, Vol. 2, ed. David Kerekes. Criticial Vision/Headpress, 2005.

"Representing Atrocity: From the Holocaust to September 11," in *Film and Television After 9/11*, ed. Wheeler Winston Dixon. Southern Illinois University Press, 2004.

"*Shadow of the Vampire*," in *Film Review Annual: 2001— Films of 2000*, ed. Jerome Ozer. Film Review Publications, 2004.

"*Fargo* in Context: The Middle of Nowhere?" in *The Coen Brothers' Fargo*, ed. William Luhr. Cambridge University Press, 2003.

"*The Wrong Man*," in *The Hidden God*, ed. Mary Lea Bandy and Antonio Monda. The Museum of Modern Art, 2003.

"*L'Humanité*," written with Mikita Brottman, in *The Hidden God*, ed. Mary Lea Bandy and Antonio Monda. The Museum of Modern Art, 2003.

Multiple Titles, *The 1,001 Films You Must See Before You Die*, ed. Steven Schneider. Quintet, 2003.

"Hitchcock, Bakhtin, and the Carnivalization of Cinema" and "Alfred Hitchcock: Registrar of Births and Deaths," in *Framing Hitchcock: Selected Essays from the Hitchcock Annual*, ed. Sidney Gottlieb and Christopher Brookhouse. Wayne State University Press, 2002.

"*Breathless*" and "*Nashville*" and "*Do the Right Thing*," in *The A List: The National Society of Film Critics' 100 Essential Films*, ed. Jay Carr. Da Capo, 2002.

"The Personal Is Political for a Chinese Director," in *Zhang Yimou: Interviews*, ed. Frances Gateward. University Press of Mississippi, 2001.

"Thanatos ex Machina: Godard Caresses the Dead," in *Car Crash Culture*, ed. Mikita Brottman. Palgrave/ St. Martin's Press, 2001.

"Mike Leigh Calls It as He Sees It," in *Mike Leigh: Interviews*, ed. Howie Movshovitz. University Press of Mississippi, 2000.

"Jane Campion Directs on Instinct," in *Jane Campion: Interviews*, ed. Virginia Wright Wexman. University Press of Mississippi, 1999.

"Notes: Meredith Monk," in *Meredith Monk*, ed. Deborah Jowitt. Johns Hopkins University Press, 1997.

"Miéville and Godard: From Psychology to Spirit," in *Jean-Luc Godard's* Hail Mary: *Women and the Sacred in Film*, ed. Maryel Locke and Charles Warren. Southern Illinois University Press, 1993.

"Robert Altman," in *American Directors*, ed. Jean-Pierre Coursodon. McGraw-Hill, 1983.

"Motion Pictures," in *Funk & Wagnalls New Encyclopedia Yearbooks*, ed. Albert Bennett and Robert Halasz. Funk & Wagnalls, 1979, 1980, 1981, 1982, 1983.

DVD & Blu-ray commentaries, essays, appearances

Audio Commentary, Sympathy for the Devil/One Plus One, Abkco, 2018.

"Guerrilla Fantasy," Booklet Essay for *Time Bandits*, The Criterion Collection, 2014.

"Too Late Blues," Booklet Essay for *Too Late Blues*, Masters of Cinema, UK, 2014.

"A Timeless History," Booklet Essay for *A Brief History of Time*, The Criterion Collection, 2014.

"Breaking the Rules," Booklet Essay for *Breaking the Waves*, The Criterion Collection, 2014.

"Reborn Again," Booklet Essay for *Seconds*, The Criterion Collection, 2013.

"Life Is Bittersweet," Booklet Essay for *Life Is Sweet*, The Criterion Collection, 2013.

"*The White Shadow*," DVD and Booklet Essay for "Lost and Found: American Treasures from the New Zealand Film Archive," National Film Preservation Foundation, 2013.

"*Brazil*: A Great Place to Visit, Wouldn't Want to Live There," Booklet Essay for *Brazil*, The Criterion Collection, 2012.

"All in the Game," Booklet Essay for *The Game*, The Criterion Collection, 2012.

"Wars on Terror," Booklet Essay for *Life During Wartime*, The Criterion Collection, 2011.

Appearance, *The Master's Touch: Hitchcock's Signature Style*, in *North by Northwest*, 50th Anniversary Edition, Warner Home Video, 2010.

"This Side of Paradise," Booklet Essay for *The Thin Red Line*, The Criterion Collection, 2010.

Appearance, *Jean-Luc Godard: A Riddle Wrapped in an Enigma*, in *The Jean-Luc Godard Box Set*, Lionsgate, 2008.

Appearance, *Pure Cinema: Through the Eyes of the Master*, in *Rear Window*, Universal Legacy Series, 2008.

Appearance, *Breaking Barriers: The Sound of Hitchcock*, in *Rear Window*, Universal Legacy Series, 2008.

Appearance, *Partners in Crime; Hitchcock's Collaborators*, in *Rear Window*, Universal Legacy Series, 2008.

"War and Peace," Booklet Essay for *The Two of Us*. The Criterion Collection, 2007.

"Wake Up!" Booklet Essay for *Sweet Movie*, The Criterion Collection, 2007.

Audio Commentaries and Essay. *Essential Directors Series— Jean-Luc Godard*, Wellspring Media, 2007.

Audio Commentary and Essay, *Weekend*, New Yorker Video, 2005.

Notre Musique, Essay for Wellspring, 2005.

"*3 Women*: Dream Project," Booklet Essay for *3 Women*, The Criterion Collection, 2004.

Audio Commentary, *Breathless*, Winstar TV and Video, 2001.

Audio Commentary, *Le Petit Soldat*, Winstar TV and Video, 2001.

Audio Commentary, *Les Carabiniers*, Winstar TV and Video, 2001.

INDEX

www.ingramcontent.com/pod-product-compliance
Lightning Source LLC
Chambersburg PA
CBHW060417130626
46555CB00005B/2104